SPEAK UP

SPEAK UP

UNSILENCING THE VOICES
OF ASIAN AMERICANS

PAIGE YANG

SPEAK UP

Unsilencing the Voices of Asian Americans

ISBN   978-1-64137-368-5   *Paperback*

            978-1-64137-716-4   *Ebook*

This book is affectionately dedicated to Mary C. Lydon, a parent to me and a friend to all, who ignited the writer in me.

CONTENTS

ACKNOWLEDGEMENTS

———

Along my journey in writing this book, I had the unique opportunity to interview individuals from all over the country. Each conversation, whether told through anonymous stories or in person, gave me a glimpse into the severity of the mental health crises in the Asian American community. I am grateful to family, friends, and strangers who made this book possible. Through writing *Speak Up: Unsilencing the Voices of Asian Americans,* I've discovered that it truly takes a village to publish a book.

First and foremost, I'd like to thank my fiancé, Allen, who supported me through every step of the way and gave me the courage to take on this opportunity to fulfill my dream. Thank you to my parents who inspire me every day with their strong work ethic. And thank you, my incredible editors,

Clayton Bohle and Linda Berardelli, for seeing the worst of my work and still believing in me.

Thank you, my cover designer, Milos Mandic, for being so patient in working with me to create a cover that reflects the core elements of the book. And to *New Degree Press*, especially Eric Koester and Brian Bies, for instilling confidence in me and for sacrificing countless hours of sleep to ensure that the stories in my book are heard.

And a huge thank you to everyone who gave me their time for a personal interview, pre-ordered the eBook, paperback, and multiple copies to make publishing possible, helped spread the word about *Speak Up: Unsilencing the Voices of Asian Americans* to gather amazing momentum, and help me publish a book I am proud of. I am sincerely grateful for all of your help.

Here are the individuals who have been part of my journey:

Allen Cai

Anonymous Storytellers

Kim Espinosa

Victoria Maung

Vernalynne De La Rosa

Melissa Wee

Alina Kung

Erioapilado

Mary Kelley

Dr. Richard Nakamura

Ellen S.

Viviane Hoang

Emily Wu Truong

Amy Wang

G.L.

Ruby Chi

Tessa Garcia

Manal Saleh

Jing Yang

Kay-Anne Reed

Jennifer Cheang

Y.X.L.

Jeff Han

Michael Huynh

HACKING THIS BOOK

THE STRUCTURE OF THE BOOK

This book does not have to be read in order. You may pick and choose the chapters based on who you are and where you are in life. Many chapters are connected and individuals may be referenced in more than one chapter. However, you do not have to read the book from cover to cover. You may jump to any chapter that interests you.

IDENTIFY WHAT YOU HOPE TO LEARN FROM THIS BOOK

Although there are only ten chapters to this book, having a clear goal can be helpful when reading through the novel. For general readers and particularly those unfamiliar with this topic, this book advocates for a better understanding of the impact of culture and with it, stigma and shame, on the underutilization of mental health services in Asian Americans. For Asian Americans living with mental illnesses, the goals of this book are for you to know that you are not alone in this journey and that there is nothing shameful about living with mental disorders.

This book, for those who know of family and or friends living with mental disorders, seeks to help them understand the complex layers of barriers that impact the quality of life of Asian Americans and their overall health outcome. And for health care professionals, the hope is that gaining a deeper understanding of these barriers will help to galvanize an increased effort to enhance cultural competency in the healthcare field so as to truly provide patient-centered care.

SUGGESTED READING GUIDE

FOR THE GENERAL READER

- Introduction
- Chapter 2: Not a Model—Just a Minority
- Chapter 6: Mind Over Body: How Our Brain Controls the Body

- Chapter 8: The Unsung Heroes
- Chapter 9: An Uphill Battle: The Role of Local and National Organizations
- Chapter 10: What's Next?

FOR ASIAN AMERICANS LIVING WITH MENTAL DISORDERS

- Introduction
- Chapter 3: Be Selfish
- Chapter 4: You Matter
- Chapter 5: There is Hope
- Chapter 6: Mind Over Body: How Our Brain Controls the Body
- Chapter 7: Finding Your Match
- Chapter 10: What's Next?

FOR FAMILY AND FRIENDS

- Introduction
- Chapter 1: Save the Person, Not the Face
- Chapter 2: Not a Model—Just a Minority
- Chapter 6: Mind Over Body: How Our Brain Controls the Body
- Chapter 10: What's Next?

FOR HEALTH CARE PROFESSIONALS

- Introduction
- Chapter 2: Not a Model—Just a Minority
- Chapter 6: Mind Over Body: How Our Brain Controls the Body
- Chapter 7: Finding Your Match
- Chapter 8: The Unsung Heroes
- Chapter 9: An Uphill Battle: The Role of Local and National Organizations
- Chapter 10: What's Next?

INTRODUCTION

———

Shame. Disgrace.

That was how an anonymous storyteller's parents viewed her. At least, before she proved herself worthy after attaining what was considered "successful" in her parents' eyes.

> *"I didn't fully grasp what depression, anxiety and all that was until I was maybe in my teens but I suspected that I've always struggled with it at an early age. I was born in Hong Kong to parents from the Philippines who moved to HK. At three months old (or roughly around that time), I moved to the Philippines fo [sic] live with my grandma—she raised me. I never met my parents until I was about 5-6 when I moved back to HK. Needless to say, I has [sic] to*

live with them who were complete strangers," shared
the storyteller.

She continued:

"I suffered abuse from my mom when I was growing
up. She would often slap me, push me or hit me with
a bottle or a chair because I was a "noisy" kid. I have
two brothers who never experienced this. Because of
this, I think I was forced fo [sic] grow up. My tiny
mind had to understand why I was being treated
this way and I began to lose trust in other people
so I "raised" myself. I became more aware of what
I should do or shouldn't do, I control how I act and
what I say. During my teens (late elementary to fresh-
men year of high school), my physical abuses turn to
emotional abuse."

But despite the unimaginable physical, psychological, and
emotional abuse from her biological mother, she continued
to yearn for her attention, acceptance, and love.

In Chapter 1 we will embark on a short journey with the
storyteller that is filled with pain, toxic relationships,
and eventually finding the help that she so desperately
needed in order to heal from the decades of trauma and
self-hatred.

While no two stories are the same, the fear of shame and bringing disgrace upon the family name along with the prioritization of "success" in the eyes of her parents is a common theme found among the stories told by numerous Asian Americans who struggled with and delayed their treatment for mental illnesses.

Listening to and reading through one heartbreaking story after another *and* another of Asian Americans' experiences living with mental illnesses it is evident that the stigma against mental disorders is as much a part of our communities as our cultures are. Intertwined with the pervasive nature of this stigma is the concept of saving face.

**

What do you want to be when you grow up?

"I want to be an artist!" I responded excitedly.

"You know what happens to artists? They only make money *after* they die."

That was what my mom told me when I was eight years old. Needless to say, I quickly dropped that dream. As a child, the mere mention of death was enough to make me run in the other direction, and even though I may have missed her point, it still convinced me to seek a different career. That career turned out to be a registered nurse.

I am fortunate to be in a career field that I am passionate about and that allows me to help others, while still being able to do art as a hobby. But as I've grown older and had time to reflect on my childhood, I think back to that pivotal moment.

Was my mom trying to save me from pursuing a stereotypically jobless career? Or was she trying to save face and keep me from bringing shame to the family?

With plans for a brighter future for their children, Asian parents implement a strict set of disciplinary rules and pre-scheduled events on their child's timeline called, "life," so that no opportunities are missed. This type of parenting style has been notoriously labeled as "tiger parenting," which started gaining polarized feedback since Amy Chua's controversial book, *Battle Hymn of the Tiger Mother*. Newspapers across the country also published articles about her family life and parenting style, like when she denied her daughters from attending sleepovers and chose her daughters' course schedules. Many of these parents are living the American dream, the life they never had, through their children and yet are not letting their children live their own lives.

After reading various newspaper articles on Amy Chua's parenting style, I realized that I grew up with a variation of a tiger mom. I remember on Sundays when my parents were off from work, they would bring out their dusty, gigantic dictionary. Three of my siblings and I had to write down the words along with the definitions starting from the letter "A." In response to our complaints, my parents reassured us by sharing that they knew of a Korean couple that made their children kneel on the floor while memorizing words and their children are now successful doctors. Yes, very reassuring. At least we didn't have to kneel on the floor because we had seats to sit on.

**

Mental health is no exception when it comes to saving face and bringing shame to the family. So much shame and stigma exist within the Asian community that it is preventing individuals from seeking the help they so desperately need in order to live a full and healthy life. I wanted to write this book because I want to advocate for mental health wellness through raising awareness and by extension, normalizing mental health and reducing the stigma surrounding it.

Working in the healthcare field, I had no doubt that mental illnesses exist. Courses in psychology, pathophysiology, anatomy and physiology, and pharmacology; clinical rotation on a mental health ward; and working with patients with mental disorders as one of their many health comorbidities proved enough evidence that mental illnesses exist.

But it wasn't until I started volunteering at the Midwest Asian Health Association, a local non-profit organization that caters to the healthcare needs of Chinese Americans that I started hearing and learning about the prevalence of mental illnesses in this community. When I worked on the suicide and bullying grant, I became aware of the paucity of data on Asian Americans. Finding data on the prevalence of suicide, for example, among Chinese Americans versus Hmong Americans versus Indian Americans, proved extremely difficult. This may be caused by the design of research surveys in which all ethnicities within the continent of Asia is viewed as a monolithic group, thus failing to take into account of the diversity under the umbrella term. And in doing so, such surveys indirectly negate the polarizing experiences of, for example, Korean Americans versus Cambodian Americans.

I thought to myself, do we not matter?

I was surprised by the lack of outreach effort, research, and awareness that had been done on Asian Americans. But maybe I should not be so surprised after all, considering mental health is often a taboo subject even at home. Growing up, I remember hearing stories from the region that my family is from and how individuals are unable to find marriage partners because of rumors about an extended family member being "crazy." There is so much fear and stigma around mental disorders.

- Fear of mental illnesses being hereditary.
- Fear of bringing shame to the family.
- Fear of being ostracized and marginalized.
- Fear of disappointment.

**

I share my personal anecdotes throughout this book because it shows the pervasive nature of saving face in Asian culture. For Asian parents, saving face has been argued by some to be even more critical than life itself, and certainly more important than mental health. To raise children that will bring pride and honor to the family name is essential, even if it is at the expense of the children's well-being.

For my parents, the fact that the Korean couple was able to raise children that later became successful doctors was enough motivation for them to sacrifice the only day they had off to make sure that we became equally successful. In their eyes, becoming an engineer, a doctor, or an accountant not only ensures that we would have well-paying jobs, but more importantly, that we would minimize the risk of bringing shame to the family. Saving face and shame are two concepts that are so deeply rooted in the Asian culture that even after several generations the concepts continue to dictate Asian Americans' perspectives and behaviors, and more importantly, their lives.

In Asian culture, the symptoms of depression are often mistaken for "laziness" and individuals are shamed for not being a productive member of society. But this is *not* true. As a one and one-half-generation Asian American health care professional, I am uniquely qualified to be able to understand the added layers of complexity that Asian Americans face when living with mental disorders. However, to gain a deeper insight into the impact of these inherited barriers, I needed to listen to real stories from real people and to find out how we can start this conversation.

Although I wanted to advocate for mental health, there were so many questions, yet I had no answers for them. So, I created an anonymous online survey and reached out to the good citizens of the Internet and conducted in-person and over-the-phone interviews with individuals willing and wanting to share their personal stories, with experts working in the community, and with mental health professionals in the field. Included in the book are stories from individuals like Emily Wu Truong who struggled with depression and anxiety and is now a strong advocate for mental health and

Dr. Richard Nakamura, who recently shared a video about his family's struggle with mental disorders and the power of support and love in helping each and every one of them thrive in the face of adversity.

Due to continued stigma against mental health and for privacy reasons, I have used an alias and storytellers' initials to maintain their anonymity.

**

It was heartwarming to receive encouragement and support from storytellers, non-profit organizations, and experts in the field. Through this journey I have found that more and more Asian Americans are wanting to speak out and share their personal journeys with mental health advocates, and that for many, therapy and treatment *does* help, even if that means choosing to not disclose your condition(s) with friends and family. Your wellness is more important than pleasing your parents, your family, and certainly anyone who does *not* prioritize your health.

This book explores the intersections of acceptance and self-care, how to be selfish so that we don't drown our own happiness and health in an attempt to save the family's face and pride, and how to differentiate between the myths and facts of mental disorders. Through this book, I hope to encourage public discussion of the factors that impact the underutilization of mental health services in Asian Americans and the added layers of complexity of cultural implications and intergenerational relationships that influence mental wellness and health outcomes of this community of over 40 distinct ethnicities. With increased open dialogue and storytelling, we can together help shed some light on the mental health issues that impact this community so that mental health can finally be seen and not demonized.

As you read through this book you will discover information on:

- The concept of "saving face" and its impact on the way mental health is viewed and treated, or not treated in the Asian American communities.
- The importance of prioritizing one's own needs and being positively selfish even if it means distancing oneself from family and friends.
- The role of local and national organizations in the fight to destigmatize mental illnesses.
- Perspectives from mental health professionals.

Most people think that mental health is intangible and only involves the brain, that high performing individuals are immune from mental illnesses, that there are few Asian Americans who experience mental disorders, and that all

Asian Americans have unsupportive families. However, through stories and interviews, I was touched when I read and heard stories from individuals giving credit to their Asian parents who supported them through their journey with mental illnesses.

I also learned that certain mental disorders, such as depression, may be able to be diagnosed through MRI scans. Mental health involves the *whole* body, not just the brain. In this book I share stories from individuals who experienced psychosomatic experiences or physical symptoms (e.g., blindness) from mental illnesses. Psychosomatic symptoms and or mental illnesses, in general, can happen to anyone anywhere. It does not discriminate and can affect *all* individuals regardless of race, ethnicity, gender, or financial background.

Even though there is still so much work that needs to be done in the field of mental health, we know so much more than we ever did. There are also treatments available for mental disorders. Statistics show that we may have underestimated the number of individuals living with mental illnesses. Studies show:

- Asian Americans are three times less likely to seek help when compared to other racial groups.[1]

---

1   Koko Nishi "Mental Health Among Asian-Americans," *American Psychological Association* (accessed March, 2019).

- Although Asian Americans and Pacific Islanders (AAPIs) make up 5.4% of the U.S. population, more than 13% or 2.2 million individuals, have a diagnosable mental disorder.[2]
- 18.9% of Asian American high school students reported having suicide ideation compared to 15.5% of Caucasians, and 10.8% of these students also reported attempting suicide compared to 6.2% Caucasians.[3]
- Asian Americans are also more likely to live in multigenerational households (26%), leading to intergenerational conflicts and differences in ideas, beliefs, and lifestyles.[4]

With the little data that we have so far, it is apparent that mental disorders exist in Asian American communities and is having detrimental effects on the community. So why do we continue to carry on this stigma and shame around mental illnesses? The brain is one of the most important parts of the body so why aren't we doing more to take care of it?

**

The most important message in this book is that we are *not* alone. By, we, I mean other Asian Americans, other young

---

2   Ibid.

3   HHS.gov, "Mental Health and Asian Americans," *U.S. Department of Health and Human Services Office of Minority Health* (accessed March, 2019).

4   Pew Research Center, "Key facts about Asian Americans, a diverse and growing population," *Pew Research Center* (accessed February, 2019).

people, other people who are worried about what people will say, or just anyone who thinks they are the only one.

If you are dealing with symptoms of mental illnesses, please seek help by joining a local support group or see your primary care provider so that you get the help that you need. Know that there is no shame in asking for help and that you don't need anyone's permission to do what is best for "you." Focus on yourself and on your needs because no one and nothing is more important than you and your well-being and happiness.

Alternatively, if you know of someone who is struggling with mental illnesses, be understanding, supportive, and don't give up on them. If you are a healthcare professional, be understanding and be educated on the stigma that exists within the Asian community and its impact on the wellness of your patients.

Life is not easy, but with the right tools and the right people, we can learn to thrive and achieve wellness.

CHAPTER 1:

SAVE THE PERSON, NOT THE FACE

———

"Smile and say hi," my mom instructs.

Not when you get dragged out of bed at 8:00 a.m. on a Sunday morning.

There was going to be no smiles from my eight-year-old self, I couldn't care less if all of the adults at the church could tell that I was cranky. But my mom was both dismayed and embarrassed by my behavior because it was a reflection on her. What would other people think of her? Uneducated? Ill mannered? Bad parenting? Low class?

As a child, I had come to be quite familiar with what "saving face" meant, largely because I couldn't help but embarrass my parents when I'm at large social gatherings. A seasoned expert at dropping food on myself (yes, even now as an adult) and a master of throwing a fit in front of "civilized" adults.

While those early experiences of being told not to embarrass my parents so they wouldn't lose face seem relatively harmless, when you are conditioned to behave a certain way for the greater good of the family, then the concept itself can have devastating effects.

The concept of "face" is so ingrained into the Asian culture that it has become part of our behaviors, thought processes, and identities. Ning Yu, a professor at Penn State College of the Liberal Arts explained in his journal article, "What does our face mean to us?" the ubiquitous meaning of "face" in various cultures.[5] Yu began by explaining that, "Our face is one of the most important parts of our body...The face is the body part that is most distinctive of a person and it is the focus of our daily interactions with others."[6] He added that the face, "conveys or betrays our intentions and states of mind...it shows our emotions and feelings."[7] In the

---

5   Ning Yu, "What Does Our Face Mean To Us?" *Pragmatics & Cognition* 9, no. 1 (2001): 1-36.
6   Ibid
7   Ibid

Asian culture, more than a display for our emotions and appearances, it also carries the responsibility "for dignity and prestige," he stated.[8] Although these two terms are not unique to the Asian culture, the abundance of metaphorical expressions given to the concept of "face" is distinctive to the culture.

Most people understand the concept of "saving face," as avoiding shame. But beyond the surface level understanding of the "face," it also represents dignity and prestige. "Dignity and prestige are based on respect, both self-respect and respect from others...But prestige, more than dignity, depends on respect from other people," Yu elaborated.[9] This means that you can lose and gain face based on your actions and on how others perceive you. In other words, face "is the currency of advancement" asserted Tom Doctoroff in The International Herald Tribune.[10]

A Currency of Advancement

This struck a chord with me as numerous childhood memories played before my eyes. Behave well in school so the teachers will praise me, but more importantly, give credit

---

8   Ibid

9   Ibid

10   "Saving Face In China." *The International Herald Tribune.* December 13, 2010.

to my parents' parenting abilities, thus gaining face in their social group. Don't date because it will interfere with our success and my parents do not want their peers to gossip about them not having well-disciplined and academically inclined children.

But as we approached our early twenties, we are asked why we aren't dating. Is there something wrong with us? Many of my parents' friends in China either have children who are getting engaged or who are having children of their own. Even now, my parents continue to pressure my brother to date and to settle down because they are worried about what to tell their friends and relatives in China. People will think that there must be something wrong with our family or that my parents have so little control over us that even their children are not giving them respect and face.

By gaining face, this social currency will allow them to not only gain dignity and prestige within their social circle, but also an increased perception of being trustworthy and honorable by their peers. In this manner, their presence and words matter more than someone who has less face, whether that is because their children did not do as well in school or they are working in a lower paying job for instance.

Therefore, there is no, "I, me, or myself" and only "us" in Asian cultures. Every single person's actions matter and can impact the overall value of a family's face, so while achievements are proudly shared, failures and shameful behaviors are not spoken of.

**

One of the forbidden topics to speak out about is challenges with mental health. To speak in public about one's journey with mental illnesses or even to see a therapist puts the value of the family's face at risk. Fear of how the family will be perceived by others, if it will impact job opportunities, and potential marriages are just a few of the concerns Asian families have. This fear and stigma surrounding mental health is compounded by the fact that many Asian parents, for example, do not believe in the existence of mental disorders.

Mental illnesses *are* real, just as real as heart disease and cancer. However, many older generations of Asians assert that mental health does not exist because you cannot physically see the damage, as you can with broken bones. Yet the irony is that Chinese people believe in Qi, or energy, which is invisible and has no evidence for its existence. My parents, for example, speak frequently of Qi in our daily lives as if it's as tangible as our hands and as real as oxygen. When I have a cold, eczema breakouts, or seasonal allergies, my mother emphasizes the importance of being well rested and boosting my Qi through nutrition and herbal soups. If they can believe in Qi, why do they reject mental health? How do we explain to Asian parents that, similar to Qi, mental health wellness exists on a spectrum and that, like Qi, when individuals experience mental illnesses, they need a similar type of support and boost in their lives to cope with this imbalance in their health?

Even though mental health is taboo to talk about within the Asian community, this existing and growing issue has to be addressed. For many individuals, the very people they trust and care about, such as their parents, silence them before they could seek professional help.

In an interview with Good Morning America, Kristina Wong, a third-generation Chinese-American was discouraged by her mother to tell others that she was receiving therapy because that may put her career in jeopardy.[11] Kristina revealed that her mom's response, "Made it clear that my joy had a monetary value, and it was that shameful to go about seeking help or even talking to someone about your problems." Wong's lack of support from her family is not unique to her. Many Asian Americans echo similar experiences where even when their parents are willing to financially support the treatment, they do it in secrecy for fear of losing face.

---

11   Chen, Stacy. "New generation of Asian American women are fighting to normalize mental health treatment." Good Morning America (Accessed April, 19, 2019).

In an anonymous online survey that I conducted focusing on Asian Americans' journeys with mental illnesses, individuals shared their very real and emotional stories. Below are excerpts from some of the stories shared by the Asian American community:

> *"In Asian culture mental health is often overlooked and swept under the rug. My parents being first generation still to this day do not understand the concept of my bi polar disorder 2, anxiety and depression. It's hard because these mental health illnesses are a part of me and it doesn't mean that I'm sick, I just need to learn how to live with it."*

> *"My parents did everything to get me the best tutors so that I could get into a good college, so that meant a 6 hour ACT prep-class on Saturday, and then a one hour flute lesson and four hours of orchestra in a different state for Sunday. It was a lot. I started developing unhealthy coping mechanisms to deal with the stress- I'd cut my shins with my razor in the shower because if I'd have done my wrists the scars would have been visible when I practiced flute. I think I did it because I was so used to bottling everything up- I think that I was more afraid of the words "disappointed" and "ungrateful" than death, so of course I wasn't going to say anything."*

"When I told my family I was depressed, they told me that sadness was only a temporary emotion. When I was molested and nearly raped by my piano teacher, no one had believed me, until the other students' parents rallied together to put him in jail for what he had done to their children. My own mother thought I wanted to quit piano and made up an excuse, when I had actually loved the piano. I just didn't like learning it for her. I had stopped playing piano since then, and I had stopped confiding in my mother of any harm that came to me thereafter. When I had tried to kill myself over and over again, I was told that I was being selfish as the knives were ripped from my hands. Before I knew it, I had created a stone mask for myself... Things have changed since then, but I have not."

"During my teens...my physical abuses turn to emotional abuse. My mother would call me a slut, useless, rubbish, not good enough, etc. because I fell in love with a guy (my first and only boyfriend thus far—I'm 23 now, I was 13 then). I was really bad at math too so she hates that. As I grew up, I began cutting. I. began to think about killing myself. I began to hate myself more. I wasn't getting the attention and love I needed from my parents... So I clung on to this guy...He filled in the hole and gave me all his attention. I made up some lie that I was dying (and also because I wanted *to) so he would love me more. Long story short, it blew up. Teachers got involved. My parents got called in. I became an embarrassment. They never asked "why" they just said I'm a disgrace. What will other people think of us parents...Those days, I felt like I was dead. I would think about killing myself almost every day. I didn't want to eat. I couldn't sleep. I cry everyday. Then one day I just woke up and said, 'I'm done.' So I did my best to be remembered as someone else, not for my past but for my achievements. This worked. But at the same time, I had to wear a mask, I had to climb the ladder of fame and forget who I am to be who my parents want me to be—successful. Now they boast about all my achievements and take credit for it when the hard work is all thanks to me. But also I kept punishing myself, I push myself to toxic relationships, to guys who are broken so I could fix them because I felt that was the kind of love I deserved from the 'shame' I brought to the family and my parents still punish me for that to this day despite all my achievements. When I turned 18, the first thing I did was see a psychologist. My parents didn't know. I paid my own treatments so I juggled working with studying..."*

There are many more similar stories from Asian Americans, mostly second generation, who had to learn to navigate the system alone for fear of bringing shame to their family or have parents who are so afraid of losing face that they forget the value of their child's well-being. What is the value of losing face against the health and the life of your own child? One of the main takeaways from these anonymous stories is a call for parents to truly see their children, to see them as a person and not as a tool for success that they can live vicariously through.

At this point, I would like to pay ode to all the parents (including mine) who made sacrifices for their children, especially those who risked their lives to immigrate to a new country so that they can not only save the lives of their family but also pursue a brighter future for the next generation. For my parents, I have to give credit to the both of them who were able to raise four college-educated students, despite the fact that they themselves never completed elementary school in China and barely speak English. Perhaps what they were showing us was tough love.

Many Asian parents perhaps love their children in the only way they know how to, that is to be tough on them and to do everything they can to ensure that they attain success in the fields of career that they know. Therefore, in their eyes, they are trying their best to set their children up for success. But success is subjective. Can one truly be deemed successful when their emotional wellness is crumbling? What good is money and saving face in the face of deteriorating health?

Asian parents know that when you sacrificed your lives for a brighter future for your children, your children also sacrificed their future for the vision you have built for them. Know that the sacrifices your "successful" children have made goes deeper than meets the eye. Below the façade of trophies, awards, and high paying jobs is a person who is suffering, and the battle scars that weep with the memories of their pain only tell half of the story. Know that your children are not only sacrificing their time and childhood to meet your standards but also their identity and psychological well-being.

Asian parents are notorious for investing in their children's education so that they can attain a brighter future than they had themselves. The irony is that their neglect and dismissal of their child's emotional and psychological health may be costing their child not only their future but sadly in some cases, also their life. If Asian parents truly love their children, they need to change their mindset of what success is and learn to prioritize the important things in life.

Asian parents, next time learn to ask about your child's day instead of their grades. Ask about their emotional and psychological well-being instead of how they have contributed to the dignity and the face of the family. Without your children, there are no grades, no universities, and no jobs to brag about. Without your children, there is no pride and no face. Without your children, there is no hope and no legacy for a brighter future. Asian parents: don't let the fear of losing face cripple your ability to hear your child's cry for help.

Surely, we are worth more to you than bragging rights.

CHAPTER 2:

NOT A MODEL— JUST A MINORITY

———

"You must've made the free throw by using geometry."

If only I had a dollar for every time I heard that "Asians are good at math" or "You must have all A's."

Although likely unintentional, this comment made while I was playing basketball in gym class stuck with me. I couldn't help but wonder if he would have made the same comment if I were of a different race. The funny thing was that I was never very good with math to begin with. I can still recall my mom stressing out because I could not memorize the multiplication table halfway through second grade.

But what does this have to do with anything?

**

To fully understand how the concept of saving face has become intertwined with mental health, we must first understand the standard of exceptionalism that has been placed upon the Asian American community, sometimes referred to as the "Model Minority Myth."

The perpetual need for Asian Americans to meet the high standard in academics is being recognized by educators and counselors. Having to constantly push to meet the expectations of being high achieving "A" students and getting accepted into Ivy League schools is causing "a lot of anxiety in a lot of the second-generation children," explained Shanni Liang, a counselor in New York City for a mental health hotline, to NBC News.[12]

Meeting the high standards set by Asian parents and by the society does not end at the academics. The model minority identity follows Asian Americans from the academics to adulthood. Asian Americans are unconsciously expected to work stable and high paying jobs, famously as doctors, lawyers, and engineers. As working adults, Asian Americans

---

12 Chris Fuchs, "Behind the 'Model Minority' Myth: Why the 'Studious Asian' Stereotype Hurts," *NBC News*, August 22, 2017.

continue to have to meet the expectation of being acquiescent diligent workers. But even as Asian Americans attempt to push back on the model minority label, the unconscious bias remains within the society.

To grasp the impact of the model minority myth, we must first gain an understanding of the origin of this concept. William Petersen, a sociologist from the University of California, Berkeley, wrote a 1966 article titled, *Success Story, Japanese-American Style,* that "solidified a prevailing stereotype of Asians as industrious and rule-abiding," asserted Kat Chow, a reporter at the National Public Radio.[13] Petersen's article pitted the success of Japanese-Americans against African Americans, many of whom lived in poverty and were still struggling against a prolonged history of slavery and racism that has led to created missed opportunities.[14]

Over time, society took Petersen's concept of the model minority myth and extended it to the idea of Asians in general being more successful than other minority groups, despite the contrasting differences in culture and experiences (e.g., immigration versus refugee status) among Asian American subgroups. For instance, according to an article

---

13 Kat Chow, "Model Minority' Myth Again Used As A Racial Wedge Between Asians And Blacks," *NPR*, April 19, 2017.

14 Ibid

written by the Asian Americans in the Law through the Harvard Law School, "Asian Americans…are often praised for apparent success across academic, economic, and cultural domains."[15] But Asian Americans are not a monolithic ethnic group. Instead, the continent of Asian is diverse and rich in ethnic groups and with that, culture, history, and experiences. Therefore, it is essential to be aware of the fact that being Asian American does not ultimately translate to individuals from that group all having the same language, culture, history, and or experiences.

**

Growing up being solely praised for my academics in some ways took a toll on my self-esteem. So much of my identity was tied to my GPA and how many AP classes I could cram into my course load. The truth was that I was happy with the fact that by working hard the results were immediate. Teachers praised me for my grades and at home, my parents beamed with pride after seeing my report cards. However, I was not prepared for what college had in store for me.

I would soon receive my first "C" at Georgetown University. I was once a top 1% student to now being average at best. My

---

15   Asian Americans In The Law, "The Model Minority Myth: High-lighting Key Stories About The Profession You May Have Missed," Asian Americans In The Law 5, no. 1 (2018).

self-esteem crumbled and my anxiety escalated. I practiced my script in my head on how I would explain to my parents that not only was I not getting A's or even B's, but a "C-."

Should I come up with this excuse, "Dad, I've been picking up a lot of the work-study hours and it's affecting my grade, I got a bad grade on my pathophysiology class?"

Scratch that.

How about, "So many of my classmates, including me, have been struggling with pathophysiology and I'm actually surprised that I didn't fail the test. I was surprised that I got a C-." I had heard that if you begin by saying you had low expectations but then you exceeded them, even a C- in this case doesn't seem too bad.

This won't work, next.

In my head I was writing and rewriting scripts to my conversation with my parents.

Although I did not know of the concept model minority myth, I lived my life unknowingly aiming to continuously meet the expectations set up by this concept.

This experience is supported by Chris Fuchs who covered an NBC News article on how the model minority myth hurts Asian Americans. He asserted that, "For many young Asian American Pacific Islanders (AAPIs), it means always rising to meet an academic bar that seems to perpetually move upward—or being afraid to ask for help in school because the model minority label suggests you don't need it."[16] The label of the model minority myth means that you should and can succeed without asking for help and if you do ask for help, it is a sign of weakness. According to experts, it is this created pressure of exceeding academic expectations along with economic success and in general, success in life that can lead to mental health issues.[17]

The belief that all Asians are successful is far from the truth. "Despite having the highest median income of any racial group, Asian Americans also have the largest income gap of any racial group," explained Asian Americans in the Law.[18] This is supported by the data released by Pew Research in 2019, as shown in figure 1. The bar graph illustrates the gap in income between the Burmese, at a little under $40,000

---

16 Chris Fuchs, "Behind the 'Model Minority' Myth: Why the 'Studious Asian' Stereotype Hurts," *NBC News*, August 22, 2017.

17 Ibid.

18 Asian Americans In The Law, "The Model Minority Myth: Highlighting Key Stories About The Profession You May Have Missed," Asian Americans In The Law 5, no. 1 (2018).

a year versus those of Indian descent at over $100,000 a year.[19] That is more than $60,000 in income gap between these two ethnicities! Therefore it is a myth that all Asian Americans are successful.

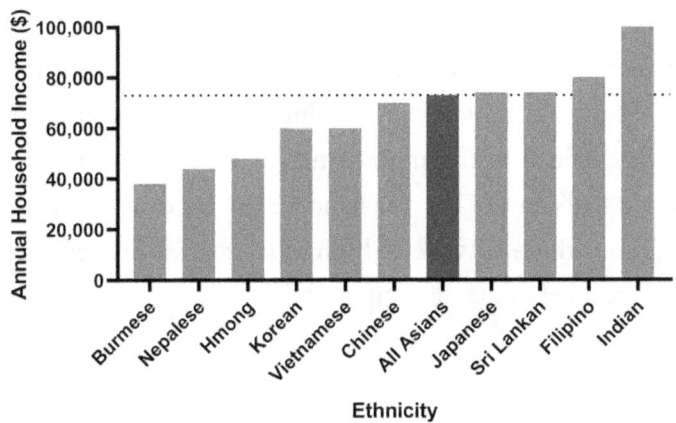

Figure 1. Adapted from Pew Research showing the gap in income among Asian American subgroups based on country of origin.[20]

A mental health study sponsored by Assemblyman Mike Eng of the city of Montebello, California also released a report focused on the state of Asian American, Native Hawaiian,

19 Abby Budiman, Anthony Cilluffo, and Neil G. Ruiz, "Key Facts About Asian Origin Groups In The U.S.," *Pew Research Center*, May 22 2019, (Accessed June 12, 2019).

20 Abby Budiman, Anthony Cilluffo, and Neil G. Ruiz, "Key Facts About Asian Origin Groups In The U.S.," *Pew Research Center*, May 22 2019, (Accessed June 12, 2019).

and Pacific Islanders' (AANHPI) mental health in Southern California and helped to debunk the model minority myth.[21] The study found that not all Asian Americans are successful and not all are engineers, doctors, or lawyers. In fact, 36% (compared to 20% of the overall population) of Asian adults aged twenty-five or older are not proficient in English and this figure is even greater among the Asian American sub-groups.[22] For example, among the Vietnamese population, that figure climbs to 53% of adults who are not proficient in English.[23] Furthermore, among California's K through 12 students, 21% of Pacific Islander students drop out of high school, which is twice as high as Caucasian students and comparable to that of Latinos.[24]

---

21 Brian Charles, "Study sponsored by Assemblyman Mike Eng shows Asian community overlooked," *The Sun*, December 2, 2010, (Accessed March, 2019).
22 Ibid.
23 Ibid.
24 Ibid.

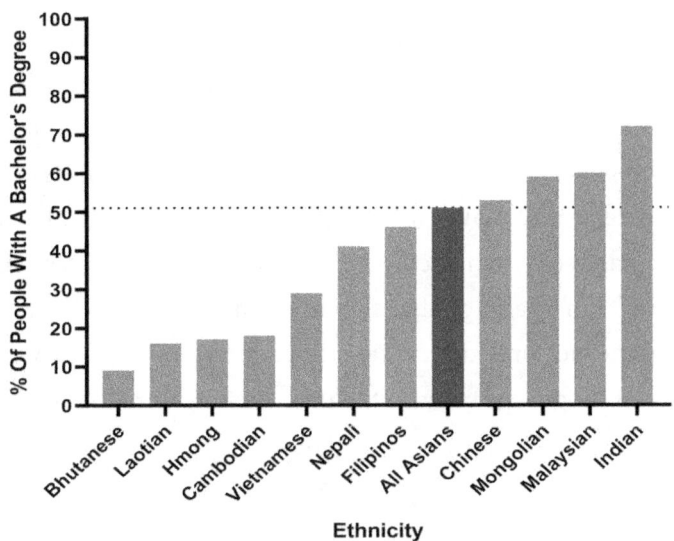

Figure 2. Adapted from Pew Research showing the gap in bachelor's education among the various Asian American subgroups.[25]

Adapted from the 2019 Pew Research report, Figure 2 illustrates the percentage of Asian Americans by their origins with a bachelor's degree or higher. Similar to the vast differences in income (seen in Figure 1), the same trend can be observed when it comes to level of education. For example, the percentage of Bhutanese with a bachelor's degree is approximately 10% versus Indian at over 70%—a shocking 60% difference!

---

25 Abby Budiman, Anthony Cilluffo, and Neil G. Ruiz, "Key Facts About Asian Origin Groups In The U.S.," *Pew Research Center*, May 22 2019, (Accessed June 12, 2019).

Despite these alarming statistics, the societal pressure to succeed combined with the highlighting of high-achieving model Asian Americans overshadows the challenges faced by Asian subgroups. "The model minority myth hides the problems and makes it invisible," states Stewart Kwoh, the president of Asian Pacific American Legal Center, with The Sun.[26] The damage that the model minority myth leaves behind not only affects the allocation of resources to the Asian subgroups but also the inherited pressure to succeed.

**

Jennifer Cheang from Mental Health America wrote in her article, *Asian American Mental Health and the "Model Minority Myth,"* that, "When your community embraces the idea that you are destined to succeed due to your racial background, failure comes as a devastating hit to your mental health."[27] In a phone interview with Jennifer, she elaborated:

"After getting rejection letters to all the schools that I applied to, I felt like a complete failure and that I was not living up to the expectations that were put forward

---

26   Brian Charles, "Study sponsored by Assemblyman Mike Eng shows Asian community overlooked," *The Sun*, December 2, 2010, (Accessed March, 2019).

27   Jennifer Cheang, "Asian American Mental Health And The 'Model Minority' Myth," *Mental Health America*, May 7, 2018 (accessed March, 2019).

for me. That I was always a step back from my other Asian American peers because I was only half...My peers [in high school] would be like...'the only reason why you're not smart in math is because you're only half Asian so you're only half as smart as them.' And things like that would stick with me, and it still sticks with me hearing that kind of information...It felt like I failed, I was never going to be enough. And at that time...I almost made a very permanent decision that I completely regret now."

With a parent who fled the Khmer Rouge in Cambodia, Jennifer did not feel like she had any right to complain about her mental health problems.[28] When going to Asian parents to talk about difficulties in relationships, school, or the myriad of topics in life, we are often told by our parents that what we are experiencing are first world problems—not real struggles. Real struggles are not having a bed to sleep on, starving to the point of resorting to eating leather and tree bark, and getting frostbite on your feet and hands because you don't have shoes or clothes to wear. The dismissal from Asian American parents combined with their cynicism of the existence of mental disorders pushes their children to have to fend for themselves and leaving them clothed in shame and loneliness.

---

28   Ibid.

The chains of the model minority label stretch beyond the walls of academics. This stereotype has come to influence Asian Americans on a policy level and on the way the health-care field and the research field perceives the mental health needs of Asian Americans. This has led to the neglect of mental health assessment and research of this group and is likely because of the following myths, as explained by Hall and Yee (2012), "(a) are a small group; (b) are a successful group and do not experience problems; and (c) do not experience mental health disparities."[29] These statements obviously are far from reality because according to a 2017 Pew Research, Asian Americans are the fastest growing racial group with a growth of 72% from 2000–2015, as seen in figure 3.[30] This is verified by the U.S. Census Bureau where it is estimated that the population of Asian Americans are projected to more than double, a growth of 100.8% from 2016, by the year 2060.[31]

29 Gordon C. Nagayama Hall and Alicia Yee, "U.S. Mental Health Policy: Addressing The Neglect Of Asian Americans," *Asian American Journal of Psychology* 3, no. 3 (2012): 181-193.

30 Abby Budiman, Anthony Cilluffo, and Neil G. Ruiz, "Key Facts About Asian Origin Groups In The U.S.," *Pew Research Center*, May 22 2019, (Accessed June 12, 2019).

31 Jonathan Vespa, David M. Armstrong, and Lauren Medina, "Demographic Turning Points For The United States: Population Projections For 2020 to 2060," *United States Census Bureau*, March 2018 (Accessed March, 2019).

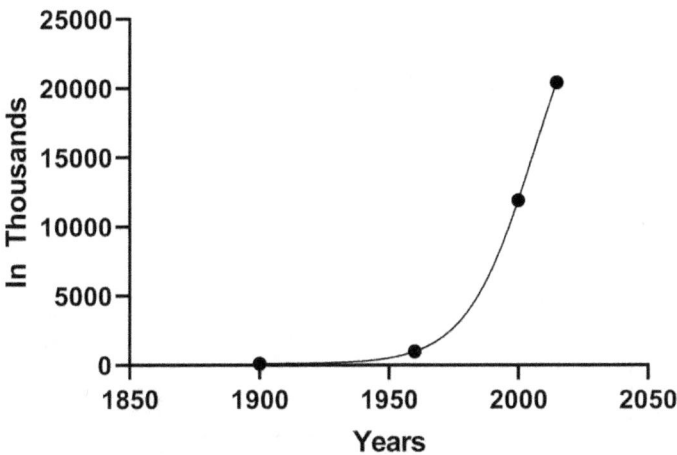

Asian Population 2000 - 2015

Figure 3. Population growth of Asian Americans since 2000, adapted from Pew Research.[32]

In terms of mental health needs, data collected by the National Latino and Asian American Study (NLAAS) revealed that Asian Americans are three times less likely than Caucasians in seeking help, even though the rate of suicide ideation is higher in this population than compared to Caucasians (see fig. 4).[33],[34] So the pivotal question is, how do we bridge the

---

32 Ibid.

33 Koko Nishi, "Mental Health Among Asian-Americans," *American Psychological Association* (Accessed March, 2019).

34 HHS.gov, "Mental Health and Asian Americans," *U.S. Department of Health and Human Services Office of Minority Health* (Accessed March 2019).

gap in mental health treatment in Asian Americans? How can communities and health care providers improve their efforts to screen at risk individuals so that these individuals receive the care they deserve and need?

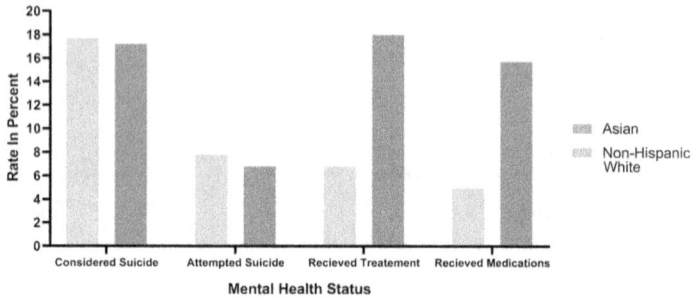

Figure 4. Mental health status of Asian Americans, adapted from the U.S. Department of Health and Human Services Office of Minority Health.[35]

The public does not know of the dire mental health needs of Asian Americans because the expectations and responsibilities that come with the model minority myth has existed for so long that it has become a part of our identities. To stray off the path that society has drawn for us and not to conform to the norm may mark individuals as outcasts of the community. But from the stories shared in this book and beyond, we know that there are many more Asian Americans who have

_____

35   Ibid.

experience with mental illnesses than reported in research. The question is how do we break the silence? How do we break free of the chains of the responsibility that comes with simply being Asian American? There is still so much work that needs to be done if we want to unchain the weight of the model minority myth. The first step is for us to share our stories so that collectively we can be heard and unsilenced.

CHAPTER 3:

BE SELFISH

Stemming from the same concept of saving face is the idea in many Asian cultures that there is no "you or I," only "us."

There is no individualism.

An individual's actions reflect on the whole family and community, not just the person herself or himself. For example, there is an idiom in Japanese that translates to English as, "The nail that sticks out gets hammered down." This saying illustrates the consequences of deviating from the norm. You could be singled out if you act differently and don't meet societal expectations. This cumbersome and culturally inherited responsibility of scrutinizing one's own actions before acting has had and continues to have a destructive impact on the well-being of Asian Americans.

At a young age, we learned to not be selfish because it reflects poorly, not only on ourselves but also our parents. We practice filial piety at a young age and learned to always place the needs of others and the family above our own, and all while keeping in mind the impact of our actions on the image of the family. This places a tremendous amount of pressure on Asian Americans, regardless of whether you are a first or a second generation Asian American.

Growing up I recall hearing stories of how certain families are looked down on, not because of what they did, but instead what their grandparents, great aunt, or extended families did. For example, if someone's great uncle was put in jail for robbery, his actions now have put the reputation of his immediate and extended family in jeopardy. When anyone related to him wishes to get married, they are going to have a tough time because no family wants to be associated with the bad reputation or the risk of inheriting the "bad genes." This was especially prevalent in the past when families used to live in the same neighborhood or village for multiple generations and everyone knew everyone else's business. There was no way to escape gossip.

At home, mastering the art of keeping family business within the immediate family is highly praised. My mom would always look up to people who can navigate a conversation without leaking information about the true nature of how their family is doing. To openly share information with people outside of the family is frowned upon and seen as an immature adult. I remember on multiple occasions where my parents would get upset when I told them about the things I talked about with people I dated or with my close friends. They would comment, "Why did you tell them that? You shouldn't share these kinds of things with other people."

It seemed to me and still seems perfectly acceptable to share with close friends if someone in my family underwent rotator cuff surgery or a sibling finished college in more than four years because of certain life and medical events. I would share family events such as these with close friends and people I trust, not strangers. But still, in their eyes, I should not have.

I can recall more often than not, the things I shared with others were insignificant and wouldn't tarnish our family image, but to my parents, if you can share as little as you can, that is the way to go. Because the less you talk, the less likely you will leak unnecessary information about your family, thus risking the family image that they have worked so hard to maintain.

Funny enough, just the other day, my mom called me halfway across the country to remind me to not talk about a certain topic.

I was twenty-five years old.

It seems that age doesn't matter. If you are part of the family, it does not matter if you are eighty years old or one-hundred years old, you have to make sure your actions and words reflect on the family well.

Andrew Min, a Korean-American, can relate to the concept of an individual's responsibility to uphold the image of the family.[36] He shared his journey with mental illness through *Erasing Shame*, a podcast that strives to erase shame through honest talk for healthy living.[37] He explained that there is "almost a standard of perfection…no flaws thing that every Asian American family wants to look to, and then they impose it on their kids…if you don't do that then you are failing me."[38]

Andrew recalled being sensitive to the needs of others even at an early age when he noticed that his parents were not having their needs met by each other. In an interview with, *Erasing Shame*, Andrew shared that his parents got divorced when he was in fourth grade.[39] Growing, he felt that he was

---

36   "Korean American Pressures To Be Perfect." *Erasing Shame* (blog). July 5, 2018.

37   "About." *Erasing Shame* (blog). n.d.

38   "Korean American Pressures To Be Perfect." *Erasing Shame* (blog). July 5, 2018.

39   Ibid.

"walking on eggshells a lot of time" and couldn't remember much other than "this vague sense of sadness, like okay my home was unhappy."[40] But despite an unhappy childhood, he was very sensitive to other people's happiness.

He elaborated that "there's a different kind of pressure that comes in Asian American families that is a lot more painful or difficult" because for example, if the child acts out, it looks bad on the parents; and if the child made "other people uncomfortable, they're looking at me (the parent[s]) and think that I'm doing something wrong or failing as a parent."[41]

It wasn't until later when Andrew worked with foster youths and was being trained in dealing with childhood trauma and behavioral disorders that he learned the importance of establishing a healthy home environment to raise children.[42] He started getting flashbacks from his childhood and the pieces of the puzzle started to fit together.[43]

Although he did not experience domestic violence, there was "a lot of emotional neglect, a lot of emotional abuse a lot of...unhappiness. I've been around, even substance

---

40 Ibid.
41 Ibid.
42 Ibid.
43 Ibid.

abuse."[44] What stood out for him during the training was the keyword, "child."[45] He stated, "When a baby cries out and a parent responds, the child begins to learn that their voice matters."[46]

This powerful insight triggered his memory of waking up one evening hearing his mom in the kitchen crying on the phone arguing with his dad and later breaking down weeping on the floor.[47] Not knowing what to do, he ran to his room and cried out "mom, mom, mom" he recalled.[48] Andrew didn't know what to say but wanted her to come and comfort him and tell him that everything was going to be okay.[49]

He continued, "I'm crying and crying and she never showed up. And I spent maybe 30 minutes—an hour—crying for my mom to come and she never came."[50] He then heard his mom close her door.[51] At that moment, "I tell myself that my voice doesn't matter, that their needs are more important than my needs and unless people are happy and okay, then everything's wrong" Andrew shared.[52]

---

44   Ibid.
45   Ibid.
46   Ibid.
47   Ibid.
48   Ibid.
49   Ibid.
50   Ibid.
51   Ibid.
52   Ibid.

After that event, Andrew started to believe that his needs are secondary to other peoples' needs and that if he can make sure that they are happy, he'll also be happy.[53]

But this was not the case.

When he grew up, even when others praised him and told him how proud they were of him as a youth pastor, he felt miserable.[54] He felt stressed and trapped inside a façade that he had created. Andrew reflected, "I felt like an imposter. I felt like I was failing. I felt like I had to prove myself at maintaining this image."[55] The increasing pressure to perform and the crippling fear of disappointing everyone around him finally broke him.[56] Not having told anyone but his pastor, he went ahead and bought himself a one-way ticket to Korea.[57] Later he would decide to return to the States and reveal to others of what he had been going through and of his fears, insecurities, and flaws.[58] To his surprise, the people around him were not only accepting of his flaws and limitations but were already aware of them and have embraced him for whom he was and is.[59]

---

53 Ibid.
54 Ibid.
55 Ibid.
56 Ibid.
57 Ibid.
58 Ibid.
59 Ibid.

Andrew supported that "there definitely is a stigma, a fear of showing weakness in the Asian American community and I think parts of it are rooted in again back into how the corporate identity of your actions reflect on us."[60] In Asian cultures, it's never about you, it's about the family and it's about the community that you're part of. And over time, the mentality of being part of a whole, and the ripple effect of our actions have caused many Asian Americans to become fearful of being selfish. Andrew asserted, "For you to express the fact that you have needs, that there's something that you feel is lacking is so selfish."[61]

The negative association between expressing our needs and being selfish deters Asian Americans from seeking help. As Andrew and many anonymous storytellers have said, because of the stigma against mental health, for an individual to ask for help would mean that the individual is both weak and selfish. Focusing on the needs of their own and putting the image of their family at risk would be selfish.

But Asian Americans need to learn to be selfish.

We need to learn to focus on ourselves, especially on our well-being. The journey to self-care may be challenging

---

60 Ibid.
61 Ibid.

because we are so accustomed to suppressing our individual needs that we don't know when we need help. Andrew confessed, "I feel like I sound crazy when I say this. I become so unaware of my own needs that I don't know when I'm tired. I don't know when I'm hungry. I don't know when I'm thirsty. It's like I don't feel it until it gets extreme."[62]

Many Asian Americans do not seek help until the symptoms have become moderate or severe, which is why it's so important for communities and health care organizations to implement Mental Health America's B4Stage 4 initiative. This initiative explains that mental health is health on a spectrum and should be viewed as any other socially accepted health issues, such as heart disease and skin cancer.[63] Similar to the emphasis on early detection and staging of these health illnesses, mental disorders should also be considered as a serious health illness that requires early intervention and treatment. B4Stage 4 includes 4 stages of mental health conditions; with stage 1 being mild symptoms with warning signs and stage 4 having symptoms that are severe and can potentially put the individual's life at risk.[64]

62 Ibid.
63 Mental Health America, "B4Stage4: Changing The Way We Think About Mental Health," *Mental Health America*, (Accessed March, 2019).
64 Ibid.

Mental disorders *should* be treated like any other health illnesses and should have preventative measures implemented with the goals of improving health outcomes and reducing healthcare costs. Mental health stems from the brain, and the brain is arguably one of the most important organs in the body, so why shouldn't mental health be treated as a serious health illness like diabetes or heart failure?

JR Kuo, a motivational speaker on mental health, summarized, "There is no health without mental health."[65]

On March of 2019, Kuo presented at the Central Michigan University during the Asian Pacific American Heritage Month.[66] During his presentation, Kuo shared that he immigrated to the States from Taiwan as a child, not knowing any English. Similar to many immigrant parents, Kuo's parents wanted a brighter future for him and sought to improve his chance at a better life through strict parenting. He recalled, "Everything that was fun was labeled bad," including watching T.V. and listening to music. Growing up with this traditional and strict parenting style, lead him to feel guilty when he would take an evening off to relax in college.[67] "Growing up, the biggest struggle that I had was that I wanted to make

---

65 Maddoux Rowland, "Asian Pacific American Heritage month Speaker discusses mental health," *Central Michigan Life*, March 21, 2019.

66 Ibid.

67 Ibid.

my mom proud, but on the other hand I just wanted to enjoy my childhood," Kuo said.[68]

I can strongly relate to his struggle and the feelings of guilt when I take time off to relax and engage in self-care. This sense of guilt is exacerbated by my childhood experiences of growing up in my parents' Chinese restaurant.

BBC Stories did a wonderful job recounting what it was like for children of Chinese immigrants who sacrificed their childhoods by working, essentially, alongside their parents.[69] I remember sitting at a corner of my parents' restaurant every single day after school with my siblings working on our homework. And when it got busy, the four of us would help my parents in between finishing our homework—I even wrote my college essays in the restaurant.

We were at the restaurant 6 days a week and would leave to go home a couple of hours before the restaurant closed. Needless to say, none of us had many friends growing up. When we were younger, we protested when our parents denied us sleepover or hangout invitations from friends because they were worried about our safety and didn't know who the other child's parents were. But as we got older, not only did we

---

68 Ibid.

69 Elaine Chong, "Chinese takeaway kids: What's it like to grow up in one?" *BBC News*, January 26, 2019.

not protest against our parents, we felt guilty if we ever had the opportunity to spend time with a couple of our closest friends. We sacrificed our childhoods for the betterment of the family as a whole.

"We move as a unit, we are all part of a whole (meaning the family)," my mom would often say.

To leave the restaurant to have fun would mean you were being selfish in leaving the rest of the crew to work all the while benefiting from the hard work of others. But of course, we wanted to enjoy our childhoods, to have a normal childhood like many of our classmates. For many of my siblings, we had come to terms with the only solution that we could think of, that is, to make it up to ourselves when we grow up.

Not feeling guilty about enjoying different aspects of life is still a struggle that I have, and it has been a work in progress since I started college. I had to recondition myself to think that from time to time, it is okay to take time off to relax and not do anything. Not every action has to have tangible outcomes. I had to teach myself that having all the money, the best career, and having the most friends won't make me happy unless I take care of myself from the inside out. True happiness comes from within, and everyone, including me, should spend quality time addressing our needs so that we can achieve wellness.

We should also learn to be more selfish when it comes to our health and wellness. We cannot be the best version of ourselves when a substantial part of us, our mental health, is not well. Mental health is a large part of our overall health and we should take preventative actions to improve this aspect of our health before it starts to interfere with the lives that we have all worked so hard for and toward.

So don't feel guilty if you need to take time away from family and friends to center yourself. Don't feel guilty when you ask for help, whether that's talking to someone you trust, through therapy or a combination of therapy and medication(s). Don't feel guilty that you are putting yourself and your wellness above the needs of others because your needs take priority.

CHAPTER 4:

YOU ARE NOT ALONE

———

A person is more than their mental health diagnosis.

Even as I and part of the society fervently believe in this, the rest of the society has failed to see individuals beyond their mental health diagnosis. Mental health is stigmatized, seen as a disability and a limitation in an individual's ability as a person, a partner, and an employee. But we know that mental health is not a defining characteristic of a person and that many individuals living with mental illnesses are able to live a normal life and have gone on to positively contribute to society.

That being said, I am not neglecting the fact that mental health can permeate every facet of an individual's life and can negatively impact the way they see and experience the world. What I *am* stating however, is that part of the strategy to destigmatize and normalize mental health is, as Emily Wu Truong shared, to shed light on the "ability" and not the "disability" of mental health.[70]

Emily is a passionate advocate for mental health and wellness. She is a certified speaker of the National Alliance on Mental Illness, represents California's Mental Health Movement, "Each Mind Matters," and manages numerous Facebook groups on providing mental health support (e.g., NAMI San Gabriel Valley, Asian Coalition, and Together Empowering Asian Minds).[71] Two years ago, she also gave TEDxYouth Talks where she presented on, "The positive side of thinking about mental health."[72]

In an interview with California Mental Health Movement, "Each Mind Matters," Emily shared that she first became affected by depression and anxiety in third grade or even earlier when her family moved from Arkansas to California.[73] The move from the community that she had always known to one that she was unfamiliar with was traumatic for

---

70 Emily Wu Truong, "The positive side of thinking about mental health," *TEDx Talks*, July 11, 2017.

71 Emily Wu Truong, "Emily Wu Truong ☒☒☒," *Facebook*.

72 Emily Wu Truong, "The positive side of thinking about mental health," *TEDx Talks*, July 11, 2017.

73 Each Mind Matters, "Emily Wu Truong in Each Mind Matter's Anti-Stigma Campaign," *Youtube*, October 1, 2014.

her. In that new environment, she found herself to be unable to connect with others, leaving her feeling isolated and lonely.[74] Although she wanted to share her struggles with others, growing up in an Asian household for her meant that she couldn't speak with others of her problems because it would bring shame to her family and to herself.[75]

But then in 2013, after multiple breakdowns, Emily decided to reach out for help.[76] During an episode of her breakdowns, lasting over three days, she made over sixty phone calls to a helpline, which proved unhelpful.[77] That event led her to take matters into her own hands where Emily explained, "I trained myself to think about my abilities instead of disabilities."[78] She realized that all of her past experiences have prepared her to become a motivational speaker and an advocate for mental health awareness.[79]

Now, she continues to advocate for mental health and instills positive encouragement to others living with mental health. In Emily's TEDxYouth Talks, she shared her childhood memories where she felt stupid and slow when comparing herself

---

74 Ibid.
75 Ibid.
76 Ibid.
77 Ibid.
78 Ibid.
79 Ibid.

to her peers.[80] She recalled a classmate with the same last name as her graduating a year early and heading to Harvard.[81] In response, her mother tried to persuade her to be friends with the classmate.[82]

In college, Emily studied psychology and social behavior at UC Irvine and revealed that academic institutions teach students that, "Mental health is about deviant behaviors and uses negative words like 'disorder,'" but doesn't teach, "positive psychology."[83] She elaborated that positive psychology is "strength-based and is focused on what is it that makes you happy."[84] And that part of the effort to attain our highest potential is to be able to identify self-limiting thought.[85] Examples of self-limiting thoughts that Emily used to label herself with were that she was "stupid," "slow," and "not worthy."[86] Emily encouraged that in mental health, "When we are ready to face our fears and our weaknesses, they become stepping stones to help us grow into the person we were meant to become."[87]

---

80 Ibid.
81 Ibid.
82 Ibid.
83 Ibid.
84 Ibid.
85 Ibid.
86 Ibid.
87 Ibid.

For her, she was meant to become a mental health motivational speaker and is determined to share her stories so that no one has to feel alone in their struggles against mental health. Emily concluded, "Each one of us has the capacity to make a difference in other peoples' lives" and through storytelling, we can help to reduce the stigma around mental health.[88]

**

Mike Eng supports Emily's encouragement for Asian Americans and all those living with mental illnesses to share their stories. Mike asserted that for many societal issues, we start with the policy as a strategy to improve the outcome, but with mental health, "it's reversed...we start with our personal stories in order to get to the policies because we know the policies have not been working for some communities."[89]

Mike had previously served as the mayor of Monterey Park and had served on the California State Assembly as well as the Monterey Park City Council.[90] He also has experience working as an attorney for Eng & Nishimura, a member of the board of directors for the Asian Pacific American Legal

---

88   Ibid.
89   Asian Coalition 亞洲聯盟, "Mike Eng shares his own stories of why he cares about mental health & speaking out about mental illness," *Facebook,* 2016.
90   "Mike Eng," *Linkedin.*

Center, Garfield Medical Center, Los Angeles 80/20, and the West San Gabriel Valley Boys and Girls Club.[91],[92]

In a meeting with the Asian Coalition, an association dedicated to mental health advocacy, Mike shared his personal stories and challenges with mental health and the reason why it is so important for us to have a dialogue about this pressing issue. He began the conversation by sharing his stories, some heartwarming but many heartbreaking. Despite the challenges he faced, he managed to lace the stories with a great sense of optimism and humor.

Mike shared that when he was just two years old, he had severe physical problems that lead the doctors to warn his parents that he may not be going home (ever), but he did.[93] And it wasn't until his junior year in high school that he became aware that he was different from others.[94] He joked that, "First of all, I had horrible grades for being an Asian… and I had the worst test scores."[95]

91   Ibid.
92   "Mike Eng," *Facebook.*
93   Asian Coalition 亞洲聯盟, "Mike Eng shares his own stories of why he cares about mental health & speaking out about mental illness," *Facebook,* 2016.
94   Ibid.
95   Ibid.

In school, he painfully recalled being bullied and getting beat up.[96] Mike's claustrophobia of tight spaces stemmed from having been stuffed and locked inside lockers on a regular basis by other children.[97] "It is so severe that if I take an airplane, I have to sit on the aisle. And if I'm riding on a bus, I have to be in the aisle with air blowing down on me," he elaborated.[98] And even as he went through the extreme bullying and the challenges of being a small Asian boy, his parents were so busy that they did not take notice.[99]

Mike asked, "So how did I get from wanting to kill myself every day and being bullied and being depressed constantly to where I am now?"[100]

"I joke around because I'm still trying to deal with that depression. And the best way to deal with depression is making other people laugh; when you make other people laugh then you think well maybe the world is a little bit happier than what we think it is," he explained.[101] He also attributed his success and ability to overcome the challenges to three things.

---

96 Ibid.
97 Ibid.
98 Ibid.
99 Ibid.
100 Ibid.
101 Ibid.

The first event happened when his mother encountered a woman on a bus.[102] His mom was crying when the lady sitting next to her asked her why she was crying, to which she tearfully responded, "I'm losing my son."[103] His mom then proceeded to tell a complete stranger how she felt helpless in trying to save her son.[104] The woman offered to have Mike join her church.[105]

As Mike continued to share this story, he was quick to explain that he is not trying to convince everyone to go to church but instead to be part of a club or program that took up time because, for him, time was his worst enemy.[106] He shared, "Whether you are religious or not, it was something that focused attention on me. And something that took my attention off myself."[107] But having been bullied in school and dealing with depression meant that he also needed to increase his self-confidence and self-worth.

And what happened next did just that for him.

---

102 Ibid.
103 Ibid.
104 Ibid.
105 Ibid.
106 Ibid.
107 Ibid.

A program called, "Junior Achievement" came to his school and asked to work with the most at-risk children.[108] Mike was recommended for the program. He then met a business-man who formed a corporation and told the selected students that they were going to be given raw material and use them to build bookcases.[109] He jokingly recalled, "Bookcases?! We don't even read!"[110]

But still, the man encouraged them to make a bookcase every week and told the children that once completed, he would go into the community and sell the bookcases.[111] And in return for their hard work, he will give each child 10% of the total amount made from the bookcases.[112] Mike recalled the man asking them how much they would each make if he were to sell the bookcases for $100 each.[113] But no one responded. Mike shared, "Nobody got the right answer because we were all failing in math."[114] But keeping true to his word, the busi-nessman sold the bookcases week after week.[115] Mike joked, "If you'd seen the bookcases, you would've called 911" the nails were still outside and it was just a mess.[116]

---

108 Ibid.
109 Ibid.
110 Ibid.
111 Ibid.
112 Ibid.
113 Ibid.
114 Ibid.
115 Ibid.
116 Ibid.

Despite what they thought about their bookcases; knowing that they have the capability to make bookcases and make money from the product of their hard work instilled within them self-confidence and self-worth. Or so they thought.

At the end of the class, the businessman told them that he would host a graduation dinner for them at his home because they all did so well and made him proud.[117] Mike said, "We dressed in our best t-shirts" for the graduation dinner.[118]

After a wonderful dinner, the children were allowed to have some time alone and explored the home with the exception of one room.[119] Guess what happened next? The children went into the very room that the man advised to not go into.[120] When they opened the door, they saw that inside this "messy" room, what the man had called, stood every single bookcase that the children had ever made.[121]

Filled with emotions, Mike shared that, "[The businessman] had bought all the bookcases himself and gave us the money. That is real love. And when we saw that, we all began crying because we realized" that the worthless pieces of roughly

---

117 Ibid.
118 Ibid.
119 Ibid.
120 Ibid.
121 Ibid.

nailed wood were valuable to someone.[122] And equally admirable was the fact that the man did not go on bragging about what he had done for the kids, he kept it all to himself—at least for a while.

Even though this heartwarming event took place decades ago, the unconditional love and the impactful gesture that the man showed them remains as fresh in Mike's memories as if it happened yesterday. "You'll find that you'll make incredible impressions on people who never have a chance to say 'thank you' because they don't realize how good you were," he proclaimed.[123] Sadly, when Mike finally came to realize the impact of these people in his life, they were all gone and he could not repay them.[124] So, Mike finds himself doing the only thing he can: to pay it forward.[125]

As a child, one of the ways Mike learned to give back to the community was through the Key Club, a youth component of the Kiwanis Club.[126] He recalled having to wear the club member jacket on Thursdays, which meant that was the day he could avoid being bullied because, if the jacket got dirty, the whole school would've been put in detention, so they

---

122 Ibid.
123 Ibid.
124 Ibid.
125 Ibid.
126 Ibid.

didn't touch him.[127] But after school, Mike, along with other students were told to clean all the toilets in the churches that were within the five-mile radius and then to go to the beach and pick up cigarette butts.[128] Mike proclaimed, "Doesn't that sound demeaning?"[129]

Instead of feeling resentful, he revealed that because they were given free lunch if they cleaned it up, it meant that he was at the very least worth a free lunch.[130] The students were also made to play basketball, a quintessential team sport.[131] Playing basketball taught them the importance of working as a team and to pass the ball to another team member when you are stuck.[132] Previously, the students were on a single person team, "we were on the suicide team" Mike stated.[133] Being part of a team, you learn that you need your team just as much as your team needs you.

**

There is no better example of the importance of interdependence and what it truly means to be there for your loved ones

---

127 Ibid.
128 Ibid.
129 Ibid.
130 Ibid.
131 Ibid.
132 Ibid.
133 Ibid.

through thick and thin than the experiences of Anita (alias) and her husband, Ramon (alias), who recently celebrated their fifty years of marriage.

Although I have known both of them for over a decade now, I was only recently made aware of their family secret.

Their journey tells the story of the lows of living with bipolar disorder, the stigma of living with a mental disorder, and how Ramon regained control of his life and career with the support of his wife and the help of therapy medication. The casual interview was told from the perspective of the wife, Anita. The reason she decided to share and speak up now is with the hopes of instilling in others, who may be in a similar situation, hope in second chances.

She began the story of their journey by explaining that Ramon had come to the United States from their homeland, the Philippines, right after graduation to pursue a master's in computer science. Two years later, Anita followed and they got married. The future held endless opportunities for this young couple in their early twenties. Ramon's first job in the states was in information systems and he soon climbed up the corporate ladder, despite his young age. When his boss retired, he thought he would surely be asked to take over the vacant position. Unfortunately, much to his surprise, a new and an older employee with more experience was hired to fill the position. Filled with dis-appointment, Ramon decided to look for a new job which would take his wife and two young daughters (ages three and five) to another state.

The stress that came with the new job would soon lead Ramon to feel a sense of loss of control and triggered signs of depression. Moving to a new state meant that he no longer had the same type of support from his extended family as he did prior to the move. Ramon was so desperate to leave his new job that he was willing to drive a cab. With loss of confidence and increased anxiety, he struggled with job interviewees. Eventually, he would stop showing up at his interviews altogether.

Anita recalled feeling so worried one night when it was past midnight and Ramon had not come home. With no phone calls from Ramon, she had no idea where he could be that late in the evening. Finally, she received a call from him explain-ing that, "he had been driving around, hesitating to come home because he had already mailed her a 'goodbye' card." Anita pleaded with him to "just come home" and told him that she did not care about the card and won't open it even when it arrives in the mail. That night, Ramon thankfully did come home and as promised, Anita threw away the card when it arrived without opening it.

Later, on an evening in late October, she would receive a phone call that would turn her world upside down. She had received a call from a police officer telling her the horrifying news that Ramon was in the hospital after a security guard had found him unconscious in his car. He had ingested household cleaner and washed it down with soda. Anita rushed to the hospital with no choice but to leave her two children at home, her husband's life was on the line. Anita explained that she still can't figure out how she got herself to the hospital, especially since she had never driven into the city before, much less driving so late in the evening.

At the hospital, she felt her heart sink to the floor at the site of her husband on the hospital bed. Tears flowed uncontrollably, but she quickly told herself that she had to be strong and be in control of the situation, or at least appear to be.

Seeing Anita by his bedside, Ramon too was in tears. She heard him mumble some words which she later made out to be "I'm so sorry, hon. Please forgive me," over and over again. All she could do in that moment was to hug him and reassure him that "it's okay."

Driving home that night, Anita "prayed for enlightenment and guidance." Before the night ended, she made the most important decision of her life; she was going to stay with

Ramon. She was going to care for him and work through this together with him.

Anita continued explaining that the doctors at the hospital revealed that the lye Ramon had ingested had burned his lips, mouth, and part of his tongue, his esophagus, and his stomach. For the next few weeks, the healthcare professionals worked to drain any lye that may be left in his system. During the Christmas season, Ramon was sent home for a couple of days to spend time with the family. At that time, he was also under the care of a social worker and a psychologist.

On February 1, he was again sent home. This time, it was for Ramon to gain weight via the feeding tube in preparation for the final reconstructive surgery. Four months later, he was ready for the surgery. Anita expressed her thanks to a young and highly skilled thoracic surgeon who offered to undertake the extremely rare procedure. The colon interposition procedure would take nine hours and would give Ramon a new esophagus and stomach using parts of his colon. But most importantly, the procedure—and by extension the young surgeon—gave him a second chance at a new life!

As Anita shared this painful memory with me, I could see the events replay before her eyes. I felt my throat tighten as the memories unfolded and my eyes became blurry with tears as I imagined myself in her place, I couldn't.

I didn't know how to respond. What can you say? Except that you are sorry that she had to go through this. One moment, to have what seemed like a perfectly normal family, to one where you pray that your partner makes it through the night alive. Equally difficult is to go home to your two young children and pretend that everything is okay, that their father did not just try to end his own life, but also leaving the rest of the family behind. She had to stay strong, she had no choice.

After a long road of recovery and faith in a better tomorrow, Ramon eventually was discharged from the hospital and went home to his family. However, even after his recovery, it was challenging for him to find the proper treatment for his bipolar disorder. It wasn't until 1982 that he would meet a provider that would be able to finally prescribe him with the right drugs at the right dosages.

The delay in proper diagnosis and treatment plan that Ramon experienced, unfortunately, is a journey that many individuals living with mental illnesses can relate to. The experience of misdiagnosis is more prevalent among Asian Americans due to the model minority myth and the myth that high-performing individuals do not experience mental illnesses. However, cultural values and the stigma against mental illnesses certainly also influence the health outcomes of Asian Americans. There is so much pressure to live up to the standard that the Asian community has set up and to constantly strive to be successful in the eyes of society. For Ramon, being properly diagnosed and given the right treatment plan allowed him to not only become successful in the eyes of his community, but more importantly in the eyes of his loving family.

Ramon would go on to become the founder of a successful company. Anita joked that because the highs (mania) of bipolar disorder helped Ramon establish his company by strengthening his creative skills, Ramon asked the provider if it would be alright to not take the medicine during the high cycle. Although he enjoyed the highs of bipolar disorder, the provider cautioned against skipping the medication because you can only go down after the highs. Meaning that after experiencing the high-energy episode of bipolar disorder, there is a risk of a sudden drop in energy or diving into an episode of manic depression, which can be extremely dangerous.

Since being prescribed with the appropriate medication, Ramon has not experienced extreme shifts in mood and energy and continues to lead his company to successful milestones. He has also passed all the exams required for him to become a Fellow in his field of expertise and is certified by the government. And best of all, Ramon and Anita were blessed with two more children! All four of their children now have all been told about their father's journey with mental health and have come to better understand and appreciate him as a loving father and grandfather.

Even at retirement age, Ramon is still reluctant to publicly share his struggles with mental health, partly due to the loss of a potential client in the past. An employee of Ramon's company had thought it to be safe to share with a potential client about Ramon's battle with a mental disorder; however, he was alarmed and felt extremely regretful when the client retracted the offer after finding out this fact about Ramon.

Anita wished to share this family secret with me after hearing about this book and wanted to be part of the initiative to normalize mental illnesses both in the Asian community and beyond. I am so thankful that she shared Ramon's journey with me and through the book, with the readers, because mental health is not just a first world problem or an issue among the young people.

Anita concluded the interview with the following:

> *"As I look at my husband now — still active in his work, still able to love and support our children and grandchildren, still able to enjoy the company of friends and loved ones, and still able to savor each day he is gifted*

with — all I can say is, '...One must not lose hope in second chances."

With a better understanding of the disease, they are at peace, realizing that this was not their fault. Looking back at their life together, with its ups and downs, Anita says "Everything that has happened has brought us to where we are today. I wouldn't change a thing."

＊＊

The journey to mental health wellness is not an easy road to travel on but with a supportive community and a tailored treatment plan, individuals may not have to feel crippled by mental health challenges.

As with any other health illnesses, prevention is the key. Society as a whole needs to take mental health more seriously and see it as a critical part of our overall wellness. Health and wellness run on a continuum and the journey to achieving and maintaining wellness never stops; and for every day that we don't give up, we are working toward a better tomorrow, a better us.

Stories like Emily's, Mike's, and Ramon's demonstrate the existence of mental health across all generations of people. This is especially important to know for the Asian American community, where the stigma against mental health, like language and culture, has continued to be inherited from generation to generation. But unlike language and culture, we must teach ourselves and our communities to leave this toxic inheritance behind and to finally begin to play as a team because no one can succeed on their own.

CHAPTER 5:

THERE IS HOPE

For Ramon and many others, the right medication has had a positive impact on their life at home and at work. While treatment is not a one size fits all, especially for mental disorders, a combined approach through psychotherapy and medication can be helpful in assisting individuals in regaining control of their lives and live a quality life that they deserve.

In a phone interview with Dr. Richard Nakamura, the former scientific director at the National Institute of Mental Health (NIMH), he shared:

> "...Treatment can be helpful, can allow people to succeed. I think particularly with conditions like depression or bipolar illness, that these can have devastating short-term consequences. But successful treatment can

lead to real success...I've been treated for depression, other people in the family who have shown signs of bipolar elements, but one is a professor. So, you can be very functional, very successful, very creative, and still have problems with these disorders. And it's just a matter of whether or not we do something about it."[134]

Others have also shared their experiences with medication and therapy. Below are excerpts from an online survey I conducted on the experiences of anonymous storytellers from the Asian community:

"I am on Zoloft (sertraline) now and it's been great. Since being prescribed it, I don't get those random anxiety attacks anymore. **I remember thinking, "wow, I can't believe I feel a sense of normality again!"**... *In terms of depression, she recommended therapy but I don't feel ready for that. I understand the benefits of therapy but I think it really only works if you are willing to make great changes to your life and I don't think I'm there yet. It's a work in progress but going to see a doctor about it was definitely a step in the right*

---

134 Francis S. Collins, "Statement on the retirement of Dr. Richard Nakamura," *National Institutes of Health*, April 18, 2018 (Accessed February 20, 2019).

direction for me. I'm proud of myself for being able to ask for the help I need."

"Last year I was diagnosed with adjustment disorder with depressed mood (situational depression). **I was lucky enough to afford psychotherapy, and since I've finished my therapy sessions, I haven't had a relapse nor a reoccurrence.** *From my therapy sessions, I learned that a significant amount of my mental health issues (depression and social anxiety) stem from issues I've had since childhood, which I didn't get a chance to confront and solve..."*

-ANONYMOUS

"Things changed a lot for me when I sought out therapy when I was 18 years old and I was ashamed. I believed there was something wrong with me, that I was crazy, no one would love me, I wasn't worth anything, and I was a failure. This was because of all the preconceived notions I learned from my family that individuals who see therapists are 'crazy people' and no one wants to be around crazy people. So, it was my secret that I was seeing a therapist for my uncontrollable crying, anger issues, trust issues, and body

*image issues. **There was a lot that I was harboring on the inside that was coming out as nonsense to me, but I soon learned that everything I was feeling was all validated because there was a reason to all of it.***

-ANONYMOUS

"*Growing up, mental health was never something spoken about in my house. It was not really even until my Junior year of college where I lost someone close to me to suicide that I truly began grasping what exactly 'mental health' was and how it impacted individuals around me (including myself). In that moment, I set out on a journey to find answers, to help and educate others about the importance of mental health and seeking help - not only within the South Asian community, but within all realms around me. I began a graduate program in Counseling Psychology and... As soon as I graduated, all I wanted to do was continue my passion around mental health and pursue helping those in need...Due to my struggles finding a job...I found my self-confidence, self-image, and self-esteem slowly deteriorating. I found myself internalizing all my thoughts and actions and was quickly on the road to depression...**It has taken me a lot of time, self-reflection, and now therapy to be content with who I am and where I am (and trust me, I am*** *always working on it!). I finally got the courage to take control of myself and my life on this journey to becoming the best version of myself, so I can be the best for the important people and relationships in my life."*

-ANONYMOUS

These personal experiences hopefully provide hope to the readers that are still struggling with the road to recovery.

The journey to recovery is not a straight path but is instead filled with challenges and setbacks. The mind is one of the most fascinating and complex organs of the body therefore it is expected that the recovery journey requires a multifaceted treatment plan, one that may include psychotropic drugs, therapy, and strong loving support systems. With a strong support system of friends and family and a willingness to seek out help, it is possible to not just survive but thrive in life.

The first step to recovery begins with a desire to regain health and wellness. In other words, the individuals themselves must want to get better and take responsibility to adhere to the multifaceted treatment plan.

The other part of the treatment plan is finding the right support system, which can be a challenge in itself. Experiencing mental illnesses is difficult enough, but along the journey to regain control of life, many find their lives deteriorating amidst their struggles. Individuals may find their relationships, friendships, and careers being negatively impacted by their mental illnesses.[135] Therefore, it is critical that these individuals do not feel alone in their struggle with mental illnesses. They should be encouraged to seek out support groups and surround themselves with people that truly care about their wellness and them as a person.

Feeling not alone can be difficult to overcome for many Asian Americans struggling with mental illnesses because of cultural beliefs in the community—that mental illnesses are not real and therefore do not exist. So how does one overcome this barrier? While we do not have the right to choose our families or our cultural backgrounds, we can seek out new families and new communities that understand and support us. This is clearly illustrated by the experience of a close family friend, who wished to remain anonymous, as he shared his journey to recovery from depression.

Let's call him Michael. Michael shared that he it was in college when the symptoms of his depression became too much for him to handle. At that time, he was not familiar with depression because it was never talked about at home. Without seeking help, the symptoms of depression quickly

---

135 Mental Health America, "Recovery is a journey," *Mental Health America* (Accessed June, 2019).

took over his daily activities and he began to lose control of his life. His grades slipped and he eventually had to take time off from studying at one of the nation's top engineering programs. Even though he knew his parents would be extremely disappointed, he was not prepared for what would happen next.

He painfully recalled his parents packing up his things without him knowing and throwing them outside of the home. His parents threw him out of the house when he most needed them. They couldn't and didn't want to understand what he was going through. They just wanted him out.

Depression doesn't exist in their eyes.

To them what they saw instead was a freeloader and a disappointment—a disgrace. Sleeping on his parents' living room couch, his parents would call him a "leech" and "lazy" because he was not contributing to the family or to society. He was instead eating and living at home for free. The disappointment and the embarrassment of losing face was too much for his parents, so they felt that the only solution was to act on what they believed was tough love, disowning him.

"They thought that pushing me out of the home would somehow wake me up and make me realize my mistakes," Michael elaborated. Mistakes. His parents thought that it was wrong of Michael to seek physical and emotional shelter at home when he should have been continuing his education and if not, finding jobs.

Perhaps with the mindset of traditional Asian parents, they believed that criticizing and belittling him would make him stronger and what he needed was a slap on the face, a hit of reality. However, what Michael needed most was assurance and support from them.

Despite being casted out by his parents for fear of losing face, Michael found hope with the support of a loving family friend who he had known since he was a young child. Although unrelated, the family friend showed him unconditional love when he was at his best and when he was at his lowest. She would email him job postings and nourished him with words of encouragement. She believed in him.

Michael would soon return to his engineering program, graduate, and find a job that he is proud of. Today, although he visits his parents and respects them, he confessed that he would never love them with the same love that he has for the family friend, who was a mentor and like a second mother to him.

Michael's story of hope and of the power of love demonstrates the importance of having a support system, that family is not exclusively defined by those who are blood-related. Family is those who provide unconditional love, who you can confide in, and who empowers you to be the best version of yourself.

So, go on, seek help when you need it. Do it for yourself. Surround yourself with people who genuinely want the best for you and accepts and love you throughout the ups and downs of the journey we call life. If you were not given a supportive and loving family, create your own.

CHAPTER 6:

MIND OVER BODY: HOW OUR BRAIN CONTROLS THE BODY

———

"It's all in the head."

Individuals living with mental disorders have too often been told that what they're experiencing is not real. Not real because there is no blood work to confirm the presence of bipolar or schizophrenia. Not real because the illness can't be seen with x-rays. Not real because there are no physical changes in the body that signals there is something wrong, as there is with allergic reactions.

Yes.

It IS all in the head and there is research that supports the fact that there are biological changes in the brain in individuals living with mental illnesses.

According to articles published by the Radiological Society of North America (RSNA) and the Journal of the American Society for Experimental Neurotherapeutics, researchers have found through MRI and fMRI scans differences in brain structures, patterns of activation, and or volume of brain structures in individuals with psychiatric disorders.[136],[137] For example, in a study published by RSNA, through the use of MRI scans, individuals with depression and social anxiety were found to have abnormalities in the brain's grey matter.[138]

This is supported by Dr. Masdeu's article through the Journal of the American Society for Experimental Neurotherapeutics. In the article, Dr. Masdeu shared that in individuals with schizophrenia, results from assessments such as MRIs found that there was a decrease in the volume of certain regions of the brain (e.g., prefrontal region) as well as abnormal

136 Joseph C. Masdeu, "Neuroimaging in Psychiatric Disorders," *Neurotherapeutics: the Journal of the American Society for Experimental NeuroTherapeutics,* 8, no. 1 (2011): 93–102.

137 Radiological Society of North America, "MRI uncovers brain abnormalities in people with depression, anxiety," *ScienceDaily,* November 2017 (Accessed March, 2019).

138 Ibid.

activations in these regions.[139] The structural abnormalities and differences in brain activations are also seen in participants with major depressive disorder.[140]

So just because the brain is protected inside the skull and we can't see the changes or the injuries that it undergoes, like we can with scraped knees, it does not mean that mental disorders do not exist.

The brain is one of the most fascinating and complex organs in the body and scientists and health care providers still have so much to discover and to learn about the inner workings of the brain.

This is echoed by Dr. Lu Chen, PhD, a neurobiologist and a professor of neurosurgery and of psychiatry and behavioral sciences at Stanford Medicine.[141] At the Stanford Chinese Family and Faculty Club's quarterly speaker series kickoff event, Dr. Chen expressed that "We know very little about the brain. We know about connections, but we don't know how information is processed."[142] At the same event, Dr. Tom

---

139 Joseph C. Masdeu, "Neuroimaging in Psychiatric Disorders," *Neurotherapeutics: the Journal of the American Society for Experimental NeuroTherapeutics,* 8, no. 1 (2011): 93–102.

140 Ibid.

141 Stanford Medicine, "Lu Chen," *Stanford Medicine: CAP Profiles* (Accessed June, 2019).

142 Vivian Lam, "We know very little about the brain: Experts outline challenges in neuroscience," *Stanford Medicine: Scope,* November 2016 (Access June, 2019).

Südhof, MD, PhD, a neuroscientist and a Nobel Laureate, supported Dr. Chen's statement sharing, "Medicine is a craft… it's empirical, but we don't know how to treat problems if we don't understand the disease and the underlying biology."[143]

The little that we understand about the brain, unlike the heart, the kidney, or numerous other parts of our body, has led to the ongoing debate about the world of neuroscience on how the brain actually works. "Experimental data about brain function accumulate faster than does our understanding of how the brain works," asserted Dr. Riitta Hari, MD, PhD, in an article in *Neuron*.[144],[145] With so many missing puzzle pieces in the understanding of the brain, this has created a "separation of views which is deep among the scientists," explained Dr. Hari.[146]

All of these experts agree that while science and neuroscience have uncovered fascinating discoveries about the brain and the mind, there is still so much that we do not understand about it.

---

143 Ibid.

144 Mendeley "Riitta Hari," *Mendeley* (Accessed June, 2019).

145 Riitta Hari, "From Brain—Environment Connections to Temporal Dynamics and Social Interaction: Principles of Human Brain Function," *Neuron* 94, no. 5 (2017): 1033–1039, https://doi.org/10.1016/j.neuron.2017.04.007.

146 Ibid.

In the field of mental and behavioral health, research findings are already beginning to help shed light on the fact that mental illnesses exist and may in the near future be properly diagnosed like other health issues (e.g., diabetes). A continued research effort in the field of mental and behavioral health will help provide hope and evidence that supports the fact that mental health is a real health issue and that both we and health care professionals need to take steps to catch it early before it becomes more severe.

In an interview conducted by Kirsten Weir of the American Psychological Association (APA), Dr. Eric Kandel, a Nobel Prize laureate and a brain science professor at Columbia University, asserted that, "All mental processes are brain processes, and therefore all disorders of mental functioning are biological diseases.[147]"

The main problem surrounding some people's uncertainty in the existence of mental disorders lies in the limited knowledge in the fields of science and medicine on identifying the specific neural circuits and regions of the brain responsible for mental disorders. In the same interview conducted by Weir, Dr. Thomas R. Insel, the previous director of the National Institute of Mental Health, supports Dr. Kandel's

---

147 Kirsten Weir, "The roots of mental illness: How much of mental illness can the biology of the brain explain?" *American Psychological Association* 43, no. 6 (2012): 30.

belief in the biological factor of mental health.[148] Dr. Insel provided an accurate analogy between what we know about mental health today with our understanding of cardiology one-hundred years ago.[149] He shared that one-hundred years ago, health care providers could only assess and diagnose the patient by the patient's presentation and their subjective experiences but were unable to determine with certainty their diagnosis.[150] Fast forward one-hundred years, with the fusion of health and technology, providers are able to order blood tests, electrocardiograms, and CTs to ensure accurate diagnosis.[151]

Similar to the field of cardiology, the field of mental health has and will continue to undergo positive transformations. Take Dr. Helen Mayberg, psychiatry and neurology professor at Emory University, for example.[152] She has been working on research that seeks to understand mental health at the biological level.[153] Her research involves the Brodmann area 25, a region in the brain that has been found to be overactive in individuals with depression.[154] Brodmann area 25 interacts with parts of the brain that involves emotion, thinking,

---

148 Ibid.
149 Ibid.
150 Ibid.
151 Ibid.
152 Ibid.
153 Ibid.
154 Ibid.

and mood.[155] While there may be biological explanations for depression, schizophrenia, and bipolar disease, Dr. Mayberg explained that "When it comes to mental illness, a one-size-fits-all approach does not apply."[156]

**

PHYSICAL MANIFESTATIONS & PSYCHOSOMATIC SYMPTOMS

We still know so little about the brain and about mental disorders because different individuals may have different presentations or experiences. This is even more apparent in Asian American patients where mental illnesses may manifest itself through physical symptoms.

Melissa Wee, a therapist at the Midwest Asian Health Association, shared that, "I have gastrointestinal issues when I have anxiety." Melissa's symptoms are psychosomatic. Psychosomatic symptoms are when mental disorders manifest themselves as physical symptoms. For Diana Chao, a sophomore at Princeton University, her psychosomatic experience was demonstrated through intermittent blindness.[157]

---

155 Ibid.
156 Ibid.
157 Aneri Pattani, "She kept losing her eyesight, and no one knew why. Then a doctor asked about her mental health." *The Philadelphia Inquirer,* January, 2019 (Accessed March, 2019).

In an interview with The Philadelphia Inquirer, Diana echoed the stories of many anonymous Asian American storytellers on the question of, "How could I be suffering when I know that my parents went through so much worse just so that I could be here?"[158] To experience mental health is a sign of weakness in the eyes of many Asian American communities and families and even more so for the children of refugee parents.

Diana first recalled experiencing migraines when she was fourteen years old in a chemistry class.[159] The situation then took a turn for the worse within the course of a week. What began as migraines progressed to shooting pain in the eyes and eventually by the end of the week, exposure to any bright light (e.g., sunlight) made Diana feel as if she was blind.[160] For the next four years, Diana would go on to experience blindness for weeks at a time.[161] Her test results would be normal, but she continued to experience sessions of blindness.[162] She would go on to see specialists, such as optometrists, rheumatologists, and many others but were unable to find the answers on the cause of her intermittent blindness.[163]

---

158 Ibid.
159 Ibid.
160 Ibid.
161 Ibid.
162 Ibid.
163 Ibid.

Later, she finally met an ophthalmologist that postulated that her blindness may be related to her mental disorder.[164] Having been diagnosed with bipolar disorder as a teenager, her experiences with blindness may be her mind's way of manifesting her mental illness through psychosomatic or physical symptoms.[165]

Diana isn't alone in her psychosomatic experiences. Nary Kith, the executive director of the nonprofit organization "Kith's Integrated and Targeted Human Services," was born in a refugee camp in Thailand before her family was forced to move twice and finally settling down in Philadelphia in 1984.[166] Since the establishment of her organization, she has worked with Cambodian refugees in North Philadelphia's neighborhood of Logan and is familiar in working with Cambodian refugees who come to see her with physical complaints of chest pain, headaches, and stomach problems.[167]

Like Diana, many of the refugees have seen providers but were unable to find a cause for the symptoms. Kith explained that many of the refugees are suffering from undiagnosed and untreated chronic post-traumatic stress disorder after

---

164 Ibid.
165 Ibid.
166 Ibid.
167 Ibid.

the genocide in Cambodia in the 1960s and 1970s.[168] When these individuals were forced to flee their country—their home—amidst the war, they were often not given the time to process their traumatic experiences.[169] Being in a new country, the United States; meant that they had to focus on establishing a new home, which comes with finding new jobs and learning a new language. There was no time to grieve or process their emotions.[170] Kith concluded that, "When you finally get to process the trauma years later, it's so overwhelming you can't function," so the mental disorders reveal themselves as physical symptoms.[171]

The phenomenon of psychosomatics is not uncommon among the Asian American population. While there is no definitive answer on the reason behind its high prevalence among this population, psychologists believe that it may have to do with the stigma around mental disorders and cultural factors, such as keeping individual issues within the family for fear of shame and the fear of losing face.

Cultural factors also extend to the way emotions are expressed and shared within the community. In an interview with WGBH News, psychiatrist Dr. Xiaoduo Fan of Massa-

---

168 Ibid.
169 Ibid.
170 Ibid.
171 Ibid.

chusetts General Hospital asserted that "In Asian cultures in general, sharing feelings or psychological experiences in general are not encouraged. That's why people who grew up in Asian cultures may not develop that vocabulary to describe their emotional experiences or feelings."[172]

Growing up not talking about emotional well-being is relatable for many Asian Americans. Personally, I cannot recall my parents ever explicitly asking about my feelings or my emotional wellness even when I did tell them that I was stressed out. That was even after I first started feeling not being able to breathe because of the increasing anxiety and stress to perform well during college midterms and finals. It is not that they don't care about my well-being. Their mindset and the vocabulary they use are just different. Instead of asking how I feel about the upcoming interviews or exams, they tell me to "make sure you have enough food to eat and are sleeping enough."

The thought of asking about my emotional well-being may be unnatural to them because as children, my parents were merely trying to survive. There was no time to consider psychological well-being when there were people without clothing and starving around them.

---

172 Cristina Quinn, "Mass. Study Shows Major Mental Healthcare Disparity. Between Whites and Asian-Americans," *WGBH News*, April 2018 (Accessed March, 2019).

The lack of vocabulary to describe feelings and emotions can also be seen in the resistance of many Asian parents when it comes to providing words of affirmation and encouragement to their children. For example, my parents used to heavily criticize my siblings and me because they believed that this strategy would motivate us to do better. They would ask, "Why would the children work harder if they are being told that they're smart and amazing?" This phenomenon is also seen in immigrant Chinese parents that Amy Wang, the Program Manager at the Asian Health Coalition, worked with.

In an in-person interview with Amy, she shared that during one of the parent mentor program curriculums, she took the parents to a staircase at Haines Elementary School where each step was painted with words of encouragement, such as "you did well." But Amy faced resistance from the parents as they defended that they cannot encourage their children too much, through words of affirmation, otherwise their children will start to lose motivation and believe that they are indeed great and smart.

For Asian parents, part of achieving success includes their children to be able to fix their weaknesses. Asking for help is seen as weak and certainly so is giving in. To be able to survive through struggles and tough situations, such as mental illnesses, is seen as a badge of honor and strength.

This difference in mindset and communication extends to the healthcare field. This is especially because in this population, expressing pain and suffering is weak. For instance, growing up I rarely took any pain medications because my parents felt that withstanding pain helps to make us into stronger people. So, it was not until one time during college when I caught the flu and was running a high fever with piercing ear pains that I gave in and took one Tylenol pill. But I did wait almost two days to take it because I wanted to see if I could fight the fever on my own. This is embarrassing to share because I am currently in the healthcare field and should know better than to wait out high fevers. But growing up in a culture where having high pain tolerance is praised, I found and still sometimes find myself struggling to find a balance between the two cultures.

This personal anecdote shows the clashing of two cultures and the importance of understanding an individual's cultural values. For example, in school, we were taught that Asian patients are less likely to report having pain even when they are presenting with physiological signs of pain (e.g., sweating and changes in heart rate). When it comes to psychosomatic symptoms in Asian Americans, Albert Yeung and Raymond Kam's (2006) study found that a high proportion of Asian American patients (76%) present to primary care settings with physical symptoms of depression (e.g., headache, cough, pain, and dizziness) versus a mere 14% that describe their symptoms of depression to be depressed mood, irritability, rumination, and poor memory.[173]

Equally interesting is that none of the patients were found to consider depression as their chief problem until a depression rating scale was used; in which 90% of the same set of patients agreed that they have symptoms of depressed mood.[174]

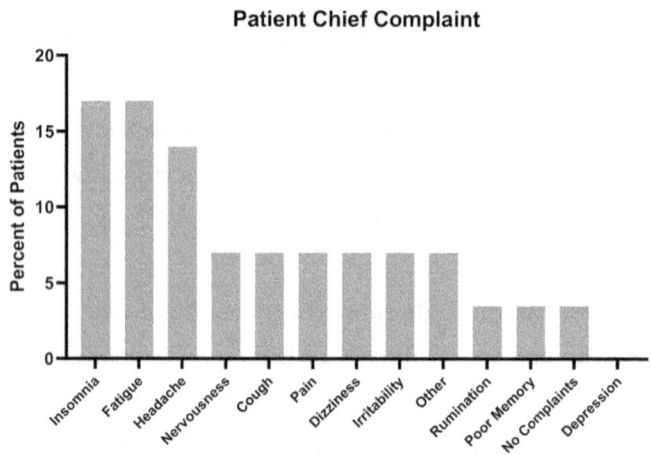

Figure 1. "Chief complaints of Chinese patients with depression," adapted from Yeung and Kam's (2006) study on "Recognizing and Treating Depression in Asian Americans."[175]

---

173 Albert Yeung and Raymond Kam, "Recognizing and Treating Depression in Asian Americans," *Psychiatric Times* 23, no. 14 (2006).
174 Ibid.
175 Ibid.

The eye-opening findings from this study reveal that when providers focus on the physical symptoms of a patient's visit, they may misdiagnose the patient. Yeung and Kam (2006) recommend that clinicians working with Asian American patients need to, "actively elicit mood symptoms from Asian American immigrants to prevent the under-recognition and under-treatment" of depression.[176] It will require training providers to identify psychosomatic manifestation of mental disorders in Asian Americans and ways to implement strategies to assess these patients with a focus on their mood rather than on their physical symptoms.

**

RECOGNIZING CULTURAL VALUES IN EARLY INTERVENTION

Understanding cultural values are essential to early intervention and proper treatment. Dr. Fan encourages providers to increase their cultural competence to improve their understanding of the cultural stigma surrounding mental disorders.[177] Additionally, Dr. Fan shared that a better understanding of the vocabulary used by the patients to

---

176 Ibid.

177 Cristina Quinn, "Mass. Study Shows Major Mental Healthcare Disparity. Between Whites and Asian-Americans," *WGBH News*, April 2018 (Accessed March, 2019).

communicate their "emotional or mental distress—often through physical aches and pains" will help to bridge the gap in mental health disparities in the population.[178]

The importance of cultural competence is echoed by Dr. Albert Gaw, a renowned Clinical Psychiatrist in the Asian and mental health community.[179]

Dr. Gaw is the Medical Director for Asian Community Mental Health Services, is involved with the American Psychiatric Association (APA), is a practitioner, an educator, and a distinguished writer.[180] In a video introduction with the American Psychiatric Association, Dr. Gaw presented on some of the best practices for practitioners when working with Asian patients.

Dr. Gaw stated, "Asians are a vast, heterogeneous group… each…with its own history, language, culture, and health beliefs."[181] Within each group exist subgroups, each with their own customs and dialect. For example, even though my family came from China, my first language was a regional dialect unofficially called the Fuzhou (or Hokkien) dialect and

---

178 Ibid.
179 Asian Community Mental Health Services, "ACMHS [PDF file]," *ACMHS* (Accessed June 2019).
180 Ibid.
181 Albert Gaw, "Working with Asian American Patients," *American Psychiatric Association* (Accessed June, 2019).

I know that even within the city that my family came from, each village had their own variation of the Fuzhou dialect. Beyond the diversity in their languages and geography are their unique experiences of either being a refugee of a war-torn country (e.g., Cambodians fleeing the Khmer Rouge) or having immigrated due to their skill-sets (e.g., scientists). Dr. Gaw explained that for many rural refugees escaping the Vietnam wars, these individuals are more vulnerable to developing PTSD, anxiety, and depression because of traumas associated with extortion, rape, and threats to their lives.[182]

Despite the polarizing and diverse experiences of Asian Americans, the media's focus on the highly skilled and accomplished Asian Americans has led to the continued lack of awareness of mental illnesses in this group.

Dr. Gaw recommends that providers assess for language barrier and use interpreters when needed; be sensitive to traditional beliefs (e.g., herbal remedies and acupuncture); encourage patient participation in treatment options; and involve family members in the plan of care when appropriate.[183] Furthermore, Dr. Gaw emphasized the importance of being attentive to non-verbal cues because many Asian immigrants, for example, view providers as a higher authority

---

182 Ibid.
183 Ibid.

and may be hesitant to ask questions for fear of being burdensome or causing trouble.[184] When it comes to discussion cognitive behavioral therapy, Dr. Gaw advises against involving the family in order to maintain patient privacy because many older generations of Asians tend to be private about their personal problems, as well as being foreign to the concept of therapy.[185]

So, it may not be that Asian Americans are resistant to treatment or don't know how to identify or are unwilling to share their emotions, researchers and health care providers may simply need to approach this population of patients using a different method.

The keyword is cultural competence.

As the population of Asian Americans continues to grow exponentially, there exists an even greater need for health care providers needing to be trained in cultural competence and to be respectful and open to supplementing certain traditional practices along with Western health and medicine. For example, providers can incorporate Tai Chi along with therapy and or psychiatric medications for Chinese patients so as to build rapport with them.

---

184 Ibid.
185 Ibid.

As the country becomes increasingly diverse, healthcare professionals need to be open to various cultural practices and to work with patients to tailor a plan of care that fits each person's needs. That is because as Weir succinctly asserted, "When it comes to mental illness, a one-size-fits-all approach does not apply."[186]

---

186 Kirsten Weir, "The roots of mental illness: How much of mental illness can the biology of the brain explain?" *American Psychological Association* 43, no. 6 (2012): 30.

CHAPTER 7:

FINDING YOUR MATCH

———

Finding the right therapist is like dating. Not every therapist will be a good fit for everyone. For many Asian Americans, there is the added layer of barrier when it comes to finding therapists. Many found the lack of cultural competency on the part of the therapists as well as the mismatch in culture to be some of the main reasons they avoid therapy. But does finding a therapist from the same or similar culture really make a difference?

"Ethnic or cultural match does make a difference, it tends to be small, but it's an important difference," stated Dr. Gordon Nagayama Hall during a 2017 podcast interview with Psych Rally.[187] At the time of the interview, Dr. Hall was a Profes-

---

187 Gordon C. Nagayama Hall, Interview with Martin Hsia, *PsychRally*, podcast audio, October 12, 2017.

sor of Psychology and the Associate Director of Research of the Center on Diversity and Community at the University of Oregon.[188]

Dr. Hall shared an analogy where if he were to be in a new city looking for a Japanese restaurant, he would look to see if the cook is Japanese or Asian.[189] Dr. Hall defended that it is not that non-Asian cooks cannot create good Asian food, having Asian cooks creates an initial attraction to the restaurant and would help him to determine if he would come to the restaurant or not.[190] Now extrapolating this analogy to therapeutic sessions, having a therapist who is culturally or ethnically similar to the client increases the retention rate, at least initially likely as a result of being able to rapidly build rapport.[191] That being said, Dr. Hall explained that over time, what matters more is not the importance of the cultural match, but rather the quality of the contents of the therapy.[192]

Despite the expertise that Dr. Hall offered on the long-term importance of quality of therapy versus finding a cultural match, individuals in the Asian American community receiving or looking for care unanimously echo the importance of

---

188 Ibid.
189 Ibid.
190 Ibid.
191 Ibid.
192 Ibid.

finding a therapist who understands the cultural nuances without the client having to explain them.

In an informal e-mail interview with Alexis Gao, who was in her last year of graduate school, soon to receive her PsyD in clinical psychology, she responded to the importance of finding therapists with similar cultural and or ethnic backgrounds.

> *"Yes, I do agree...It is best practice to provide clients with clinicians who are of the same background, but in reality, it hardly happens. In one clinic I had to work with many Spanish speaking clients, and we weren't able to provide them with a Spanish speaking clinician because there weren't any. So yes, we need more individuals from the AAPI community to work in the mental health field. And it makes me wonder why there isn't that many individuals from the AAPI community wanting to work in mental health. Is it because of the stigma, the culture shame, the family expectation of having a specific career that is not in mental, or is it all of the above and more?"*

She added:

> *"Many of the treatment models and theories used in Psychology are in a way generalized and able to use*

on any individual, but they are really catered and developed to treat the dominant culture. And many of the common treatment models that are best evidence based practiced don't take culture into consideration. So, I would like to see more treatment models, research, and literature on providing treatment to the AAPI community."

For many Asian Americans living with mental illnesses, it is essential to find a therapist who can empathize and relate to the cultural values and upbringing that a client experienced without having to explain the historical and cultural history behind these values. For example, while a therapist may recommend that a client sit down and share the challenges that they face with their loved ones, this advice does not always work or is not always possible for Asian American clients.

For instance, the therapist may ask an Asian American client why they can't speak to their family members about them suffering from depression. To which the client may have to go into depth to explain the cultural implications, values, and stigma against mental disorders in the Asian community. That often times the symptoms of depression are seen simply as the person wanting to be lazy—like they have a choice in whether or not they have the illness.

In fact, mental disorders are not recognized as health illnesses at all but is instead seen as made-up excuses for not having the ability to meet the Asian standard of success. To have to explain all of these to a therapist can take time and even if they understand this one cultural concept this time, they may have additional questions in the future. Having to explain cultural concepts along with the lack of Asian therapists are two of the major reasons that deter Asian American clients from seeking help.

Below is an excerpt from an anonymous survey that I collected touching on a commonly portrayed cultural nuance in Asian cultures: taking our shoes off before entering the home. Although arguably one of the most overused Asian stereotypes, this example does a wonderful job in showing the difficulty in having to describe certain cultural nuances to others.

> *"One time when I was younger, I invited my neighbor over (or I went over there). I took my shoes off before entering the house and the neighbor asked why. I couldn't explain why, I just did it. It was just a thing I did. And if you ask me now, I would assume it would be to not bring dirt in, but my answer would nonetheless be rooted in the fact that that's how I was raised. And because I have to deal with how my culture, how my Asianness is treated in a predominantly not-Asian*

society, a predominantly WHITE culture, I want to reduce the amount of self-explaining I do as much as possible."

This example reminded me of how I had to explain to people what Tiger Balm is and why I'm using it—yes, my mom sent me away to college with a couple of jars of it.

Even though I am in the healthcare field and can now better understand the indications of use for Tiger Balms, I still cannot explain why I used it for so many other reasons growing up. The classic Tiger Balm is a small hexagon-shaped glass jar made with Camphor, menthol, eucalyptus oil, and clove oil.[193] As stated on the original Tiger Balm website, it is indicated for the "relief for headaches, stuffy nose, or muscular aches and strains."[194] But for those who grew up in Asian households, we know that Tiger Balms have many more magical powers than what is listed on the box. For example, a humorous Reddit user by the name of "u/bbaek" shared a meme of Tiger Balm under the heading of "When your parents think these items can cure everything: stomachache, headache, bruises, broken bones, broken hearts, and hangovers" among a list of other things.[195] To add onto the

---

193 Balm Tiger, "Small Tiger Balm White—HR Ointment 10G (0.35 Oz)," (Accessed April, 2019).
194 Tiger Balm, "Tiger Balm Soft," (Accessed April, 2019).
195 u/bbaek, "The /r/APS medicine cabinet," (Access April, 2019).

list, my parents also have me use it when I have mosquito bites and when I feel bloated.

THE CURE FOR EVERYTHING

Stomachache, headache, muscle aches, cold, insect bites, insomnia, motion sickness, hair loss

Figure 1. Tiger Balm meme created by author, Paige Yang.

Perhaps Tiger Balm has a placebo effect, but it has always been the go-to item whenever anyone in the family didn't feel well. When it comes to having to explain what Tiger Balm is or what it's used for (indications from both the manufacture and the parents) to those from other cultural backgrounds, it has no significant impact on the Asian community except an opportunity to share the wonders of this little jar of magical balm. However, when having to do this kind of explaining on a more serious topic and on a greater scale about mental health in the Asian American community, it can have detrimental impacts.

This kind of explaining can become exhausting and can deter individuals from seeking the care they want and need. An anonymous storyteller from my survey and from Ryann Tanap, share their experiences below:

> "I can go to therapy, I did, but I can't seem to connect. I can't find any therapist that speak my first language probably because I live in such a small mid western city."
>
> —INDONESIAN STORYTELLER

> "I agonized over having to explain my upbringing, so I rarely participated. No one in the room could relate to my experience as a daughter of immigrants. My peers in group would question my experience and try to give me advice—and while it was well-intentioned, I didn't find their advice as helpful as if it were coming from someone in my community."
>
> —RYANN TANAP[196]

Ryann Tanap was previously the manager of social media and digital assets at NAMI and currently works as a project manager and marketing consultant, a multicultural leadership at

---

196 Ryann Tanap, "Why Asian-Americans And Pacific Islanders Don't Go To Therapy," *National Alliance on Mental Illness*, July, 24, 2018 (Access March, 2019).

AARP.[197] She was awarded by PR News as one of the 2016 Rising PR Stars 30 & Under.[198] The excerpt above was taken from Ryann's article written in 2018 for NAMI on *Why Asian-Americans and Pacific Islanders Don't go to Therapy.*[199]

In the article, she shared her disappointing experience with therapy and echoing many other Asian American's voices, she wondered if therapy "was only meant for white people."[200] Often times mental illnesses are seen as a "white peoples' illness," which compounds the existing stigma of mental health in the Asian community. This may be the result of the underutilization of mental health services and the under-reporting of mental illnesses among Asian Americans, leading to inaccurate research data exposing Caucasians as having the highest rate of mental disorders.

Based on the data collected by the Substance Abuse and Mental Health Services Administration (SAMHSA) through the 2017 National Survey on Drug Use and Health (NSDUH), when it comes to the prevalence of any mental illness among U.S. adults, adults belonging to two or more races reported the highest rate (28.6%) followed by Caucasian adults (20.4%)

197 Ryann Tanap, "Ryann Tanap," *LinkedIn* (Accessed March, 2019).
198 Ibid.
199 Ryann Tanap, "Why Asian-Americans And Pacific Islanders Don't Go To Therapy," *National Alliance on Mental Illness*, July, 24, 2018 (Access March, 2019).
200 Ibid.

and Asians (14.5%) (fig. 2).[201] The NSDUH survey on the utilization of mental health services (2017) revealed that 48% of Caucasian adults, 30.6% of African American adults, and 20.2% of Asian adults utilize mental health services (fig. 3).[202] On the prevalence of serious mental illness, adults belonging to two or more races again reported the highest percentage at 8.1%, Caucasian adults at 5.2%, and Asian adults with the lowest percentage at 2.4% (fig. 4).[203] Interestingly, when surveying the utilization of mental health services for those with serious mental illness (2017), the bar graph included data on Hispanic or Latino, Caucasian, and African American, but did not include Asian adults.[204]

201 Substance Abuse and Mental Health Services Administration (SAMHSA), "Mental Health Information: Statistics," *National Institute of Mental Health*, February, 2019 (Accessed March, 2019).

202 Ibid.

203 Ibid.

204 Ibid.

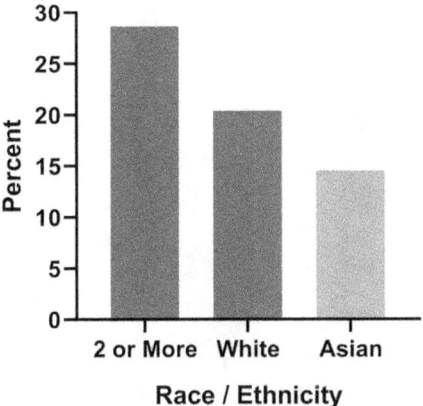

Figure 2: Adapted from SAMHSA on the prevalence of mental illnesses among U.S. adults.[205]

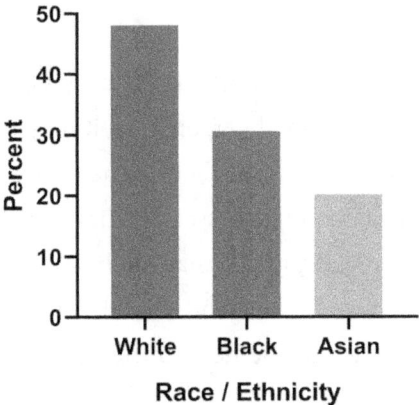

Figure 3: Adapted from SAMHSA on the utilization of mental health services.[206]

---

205 Ibid.
206 Ibid.

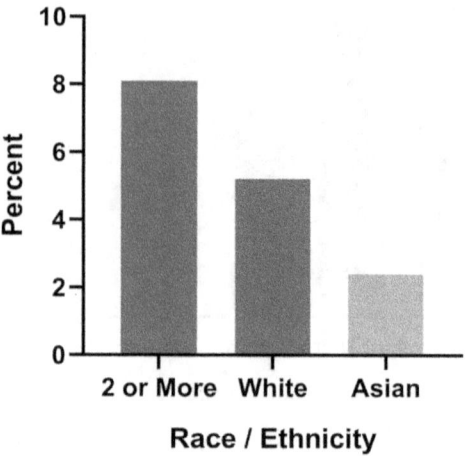

Figure 4: Adapted from SAMHSA prevalence of serious mental illnesses.[207]

While data collected through the survey conducted by SAMHSA is not necessarily erroneous, it may however be incomplete by neglecting the factors that may impact the underreporting of mental illnesses in Asian Americans. For example, the survey conducted may not be worded in a manner that is understandable to individuals from the various Asian cultures that may be new to the concept of mental illnesses.

These individuals, and even to some extent first generation Asian Americans, may be cautious about whether

207 Ibid.

or not their privacy is truly protected when completing public surveys. All of these factors and more may lead to under-reporting of data. We know that many Asian Americans have undiagnosed and untreated mental disorders. There exist numerous barriers for this community, especially for immigrants and the older generations who may not speak English.

To solve the language and perhaps the cultural barrier, Vernalynne, who works at the Midwest Asian Health Association as the substance abuse prevention program coordinator and who has a master's degree in clinical psychology *and* who is trilingual in English, Spanish, and Tagalog, recommended that:

> *"...We need more psychiatrists and therapist who speak various Asian languages. I believe this is one of the barriers for the Asian American community not being able to access behavioral health services. Therapist and psychiatrist who are not able to speak the language of an Asian client, should seek out interpretation providers who will provide these translations services. I also believe the government, both federal and state, have a responsibility to provide these costs to these providers. By the government providing financial support for these translation services, more Asian American will be able to access these mental health services."*

Mental health is not only an individual issue but is slowly being recognized as a growing national health problem, affecting the lives of millions of America's general population. This alone should prompt the government to allocate more funding to support the health of its people.

In addition to the language barrier, for the younger generation, native-born Asian Americans, and Asian Americans in general, the perpetuating cultural stigma and a lack of awareness of mental illnesses can all lead to the under-reporting of mental disorders and the underutilization of mental health services. Therefore, mental disorders may not be a Caucasian person's illness and instead is the outcome of under-reporting by other racial and ethnic groups.

As more Asian Americans come forward to share their stories, we have come to understand that mental illnesses are a very human experience and we all deal with it at one point or another in our lives. By summoning up the courage to share the stories from the community and by advocating for cultural competency in healthcare providers whose goal is to improve our well-being on the physical, psychological, and spiritual level, we can help transform the healthcare experiences of the community that we are part of.

CHAPTER 8

THE UNSUNG HEROES

———

Money and fame are not everything.

For many millennials, in particular, finding passion in our career and finding a sense of fulfillment exceeds the need or want to meet the social construct of what wealth means. In chapter 9, I mentioned that jobs in non-profit organizations are one of the jobs that many Asian parents would frown upon due to the comparatively lower salary and perception of these jobs as being less prestigious than jobs in the fields of science, business, and law.

Although the field of mental health falls under the umbrella of health and sciences, there exists a stigma with working in this field. Due to the lack of education and a negative media portrayal of those living with mental illnesses, working in the field of mental health is seen as a not so attractive field to work in. Moreover, for many Asian parents, the career fields in areas such as the arts, music, and the mental health field is associated with having lower salaries and status than compared with being a surgeon, for example. So how do we encourage more young Asian Americans to go into the field of mental health?

In a phone interview with Dr. Richard Nakamura, he expressed Asian families are asking the question of, "why are you going into something which produces a satisfactory middle-class existence when you can really make money in the business industry, electronics, Silicon Valley, etc.?"

Dr. Nakamura had a thirty-nine year career at the National Institute of Health, previously served as the director of the Center for Scientific Review (CSR), and held numerous leadership positions including being the National Institute of Mental Health's (NIMH) deputy director from 1999–2007 and scientific director from 2007–2011.[208] He confided that during his career, he had a difficult time recruiting people to go into the field of neuroscience, for example, because it's seen as less profitable and not as prestigious as other fields. He continued that this mindset applies to clinicians as well. For example, Asian parents and Asian communities often

---

208 Richard Nakamura, "Richard Nakamura," *LinkedIn*.

times ask individuals why they would want to work in undesirable fields, such as working with cognitively impaired individuals (e.g., those with dementia) or those living with HIV when one can work as a surgeon or an engineer. So, going back to the question of how to get more people into this career field that is stereotypically and seen as undesirable. Dr. Nakamura explained:

> *"I think you need to get people committed to the core problem…Helping people understand that something can be done about ill individuals within their family. Also, this way of getting them to see the broader need for treatment and clinicians and research. So almost everyone in psychiatry has some individuals within their family that made them a little more interested in that area and to try and make a difference."*

Like Dr. Nakamura, Y.X.L. agrees that "it takes a very particular kind of person to pursue a career in the mental health field" and that the vast majority, if not all of the graduate students in her program have had personal experiences dealing with their individual mental health issues. In an over-the-phone interview, she elaborated that mental health professionals own lived experiences with mental health issues often times serve to better prepare and inform them when working with patients from many different backgrounds.

Y.X.L. is currently in her fourth year of the Doctor of Psychology (PsyD) program at the Wright Institute in Berkeley, California, the only not-for-profit professional psychology school in the nation. In a phone interview, she shared her journey to graduate school and personal experiences with mental health.

Before switching her career to study to become a clinical psychologist, Y.X.L. worked in media and advertising in Beijing. In a culture that shunned mental health, she witnessed a dearth of infrastructure and resources for mental health services. But in her first year of practicum training, she discovered that the paucity of mental health resources is not unique to China.

In the United States, she also observed a lack of health care providers who are Chinese speakers or who have the cultural competency to work with Chinese or other Asian American patients. She shared that this may be "because these populations are less likely to utilize mental health services and that people from Chinese backgrounds may not be as interested in pursuing this kind of work."

While still working in Beijing, she started doing informal research at psychiatric hospitals and residential care programs to deepen her understanding of some of the mental health programs in China. What started out as curiosity led her to start a weekly group session in Beijing with a friend who held a master's degree in music therapy. One year later when she moved to Shanghai, she began volunteering at Lifeline, a crisis helpline. Y.X.L. disclosed that she decided to change her career because she did not feel fulfilled in her previous job. "It was exciting, it was fun…and at the end of the day we made our company and clients profit…but there was no meaning" she explained.

She also confided that her interest in mental health would not have started had she not been seeking help for herself. Y.X.L. shared that she was diagnosed with bipolar disorder when she was nineteen years old and a sophomore in college. During her first semester at the university, she had a hypomanic episode and did not seek help, but during the spring semester, she experienced severe depression. That was when her mother visited and took her to see a primary health care provider. Y.X.L. shared that her mother "likely knew what was going on…because her father had experienced depression for much of his life." Y.X.L. felt grateful to have her mother and particularly her older sister as a strong support system because many Asian Americans living with mental illnesses face stigma not only from their communities but also from their immediate families. She attributed the support that her family provides to the fact that mental health issues run in her family; there may exist a better understanding of mental health and the acceptance of it.

Dr. Nakamura can relate to the type of support and acceptance that runs in Y.X.L.'s family. In 2016, Dr. Nakamura shared his family's story with NIMH through a video interview.[209] In the video, he shared, "Even though this is painful, I like to tell the story because mental illnesses are still so stigmatized in our society and particularly in the Asian community."[210]

Dr. Nakamura began by telling the story of his grandfather who immigrated to the United States from Japan at the turn of the century and settled in the Yakima Valley.[211] His grandfather was one of the first leaseholders in the Yakima Valley and due to the success of the Japanese immigrants the people started to feel resentment toward them and eventually forced them out of the valley.[212] Due to the hostility, Dr. Nakamura's grandfather decided to move to California with his wife and four children and continued to farm there.[213] However, devastatingly, his grandfather committed suicide in his mid-thirties.[214] "My father, unfortunately as a teenager,

---

209 National Institute of Mental Health (NIMH), "Mental Illness in Stressful Times - An Asian-American Family's Story," *YouTube*, July 28, 2016.
210 Ibid.
211 Ibid.
212 Ibid.
213 Ibid.
214 Ibid.

had to find him and cut him down," Dr. Nakamura painfully shared.[215]

Despite this tragic event, Dr. Nakamura's father and his father's siblings continued to farm with his grandmother as the head of the household until World War II when the family (along with many other Japanese families), were incarcerated in concentration camps despite many of the members having citizenship by birth.[216] He said, "These events were thought to have been the original source of the stressors that led to severe mental illnesses in four and full bipolar (bipolar 1) in three of these children."[217] However, like Y.X.L., Dr. Nakamura shared that the traumatic events alone may not have been the sole cause of mental illnesses in his family, genetics may play a crucial role especially since other family members have also developed bipolar illness.[218]

Dr. Nakamura was not told of his family's history with mental illness until his own father underwent treatment for a bipolar episode.[219] However, he shared in the video, "Despite the fact that many with severe mental illness end up in hospitals or in

---

215   Ibid.
216   Ibid.
217   Ibid.
218   Ibid.
219   Ibid.

jail and have their lives completely wrecked by these diseases, the family stuck together, got treatment and succeeded."[220]

He went on to elaborate that despite having to live with bipolar disease, his father was able to obtain his PhD and become a tenured economics professor at Columbia University while one of his aunts was able to become a teacher and another one became a pathologist.[221] Dr. Nakamura believes, "The mutual support within the family has been absolutely critical and has been seen by everyone as the key to the family's success."[222] Later on in an email correspondence, Dr. Nakamura proudly shared, "These four siblings had successful marriages that produced ten children, all of whom developed successful careers and marriages and five of whom graduated with doctoral degrees."

Now, recently retired as the director of CSR in April of 2018, Dr. Nakamura continues to contribute his expertise and time to the scientific community through volunteering at the CSR and sharing stories of his family's resilience against mental health with the public. He hopes to go around the country telling his family's stories with the goals of increasing awareness and reducing the stigma against mental health.

---

220 Ibid.
221 Ibid.
222 Ibid.

**

As many Asian Americans know and based on personal stories shared in the book, not all families are supportive of mental health—or even believe in it.

"My Asian American family has never believed in mental health, doesn't seek out support or troubles in the family needs to stay in the family," Alexis Gao revealed in an email correspondence. She continued, "Currently talking about mental health is somewhat tolerated by my family, but only in small doses."

Alexis is in her last year of graduate school, soon to receive her PsyD in clinical psychology. Her passion for becoming a clinical psychologist first began in high school when she was a columnist for her school newspaper answering anonymous questions and concerns. Seeing how much Alexis enjoyed helping others, her Anatomy and Physiology teacher mentioned the idea of her pursuing a career as a therapist.

However, "Behind the red velvet curtain, my mom has encouraged me to be a nurse for as long as I can remember," she recalled. Following her mom's advice, she completed three years of college on track for the nursing program when taking a psychology class once again awakened her passion for psychology. She would go on to transfer and change her major to psychology. Despite her mom being flabbergasted and thoroughly upset, Alexis chased after her passion to become a clinical psychologist.

When asked about her personal journey with mental health, Alexis shared that she has depression and it was in middle school when she first thought about hurting herself. She went on to share:

> "There would be cut marks on my arms and thighs. I always wore sweaters and long clothing so no one could see. One day my mother found out my intentions to hurt myself. She hit me furiously and was in tears. She yelled, "why are you trying to leave me? I work so hard to try to make you happy and you just want to leave me." She left me in the room, and I was in tears."

As theorized by Dr. Nakamura, Y.X.L. and Alexis, it seems that many, if not all, of the mental health care professionals either have personal experiences with mental health or knew of someone close to them with a mental illness. To further illustrate this theory, Ellen S., a Clinical Psychologist, also has dealt personally with mental health.

When asked how Ellen came to choose to become a clinical psychologist, she stated, "The simple answer to this question is that I wanted to help people." But the more complex answer is:

> "*The back story to this is that my mother left my family in the Philippines when I was three years old and it was nine months before we could all be reunited. I experienced this separation due to immigration as an abandonment and interpreted the situation, in my young egocentric mind, as my fault, that I must have done something to make my mother leave. So, I spent a lot of my early life trying to please others, being very respectful of authority so I could get their approval. Becoming a psychologist fed into that desire to please and help others.*"

On her perspective on mental health, Ellen shared, "I understand the stigma associated with mental health in the Asian American (AA)...cultures...but AAs can benefit from mental health awareness because we are as vulnerable as any other ethnic group." This is supported by Alexis, adding that "regardless of available services, many individuals and families aren't aware of the services they can receive, or are afraid to receive services and to reach out for support because of the stigma on mental health."

Ellen works part-time in a college counseling center and she also has her own practice. In addition to working with college students, she also works with Filipino families who experience domestic violence, substance abuse, and bipolar illness. She shared a story of a Filipino-American woman whom she gave the name "FF." FF was in her 30s and saw Ellen at her practice in New York City. Ellen continues her story below:

"She moved from the West Coast with her long-term boyfriend and dog. She grew up in San Diego, and her family was part of the naval community. Her father was a Vietnam vet who abused alcohol and various drugs and physically and emotionally abused her mother, often accusing his wife of cheating on him even though there was no basis for this. Eventually, the mother was able to divorce him, but married another abusive, controlling man, whom she is still with, though unhappily (obviously)... The mother was never able to protect her children from her husbands. She often used my patient to mitigate FF's father's loneliness and alienation from the family by sending FF to be with her father all weekend even though she knew FF was not safe...In her mid-20's, after several stressors including having to deal with the homelessness of her father, FF experienced the first of several hospitalizations and was diagnosed with bipolar disorder with psychotic features."

It was eye opening for Ellen to encounter Filipino-American patients living in families that are involved in substance abuse, domestic abuse, and lives with mental illnesses because this ethnic community is often seen as acculturated and assimilated into the American culture. Despite Ellen having grown up with friends who had abusive fathers, many "presented themselves as intelligent and well-adjusted" she explained.

This type of presentation, of being successful and smart, is related to the model minority myth that society has created and the cultural stigma that perpetuates the shame associated with mental health in the Asian American community. Ellen explained that the existence of stigma and being unaware of mental health issues is and has continued to cause many clients to delay the treatments that they so desperately need until their late twenties or even later. Growing up in households where emotions equate to weakness and shame, the children of these parents and the parents themselves are struggling to articulate their feelings.

Based on these interviews, it is undeniable that the journey to normalizing mental health in the Asian community is going to be a long and arduous journey. Not only do we need more awareness and storytellers, but we also need more individuals like Dr. Nakamura, Y.X.L., Alexis, and Ellen to help bridge the gap in the lack of mental health professionals within the

Asian American community. Individuals working in the field of mental health and wellness should not be stigmatized but instead be seen as healers and restorers of wellness, because without wellness, there is no health and without health, we cease to exist.

CHAPTER 9

AN UPHILL BATTLE: THE ROLE OF LOCAL AND NATIONAL ORGANIZATIONS

———

Non-profit organizations: charity work, giving, fund-raising, and altruism. What these organizations are *not* associated with is fame and high salary. At this point, some of you may argue that it's not one or the other and it's not black-or-white.

True.

What I meant was that when compared to other fields of career, non-profit work tends to have a lower rate of salary than those working in the field of computer science or health-care field (that Asians are stereotypically associated with). Despite the public association of non-profit work with low wages, many individuals still find themselves drawn to these organizations for numerous reasons, personal or otherwise.

For me, when I decided to volunteer at the Midwest Asian Health Association (MAHA) located in Chicago's Chinatown, I was motivated by several reasons—perhaps some a little selfish. Beyond the desire to give back, I was motivated by the pressure that I had put on myself to do more than just go to graduate school full-time as well as from the fear of losing connection with my Chinese culture and heritage. Through my volunteer work at MAHA, I could both prac-tice my Mandarin and come to understand on the ground level the healthcare needs of the Chinese American immi-grant community. During my time there, I came to know Vernalynne De La Rosa and Melissa Wee, both of whom work at MAHA through different programs. Vernalynne has a master's in clinical psychology and is trilingual in English, Spanish, and Tagalog.[223]

In an email correspondence with Vernalynne, she shared that she became interested in the field of mental health after taking a psychology course in her sophomore year of high

---

223 Midwest Asian Health Association, "About McK-UDOS."

school where her "interests were peaked." Vernalynne credits her psychology teacher in inspiring her to further explore the field of psychology. Below, she elaborates:

> *"My psychology teacher provided a fun and interesting way to teach psychology. I enjoyed psychology so much, I majored in psychology at university. I originally planned on focusing on industrial organizational psychology; however, during my junior year, I took a counseling class. Through this class, I learned how I could help others through counseling, and I decided I wanted this to be my career. It inspired me to have the opportunity to listen to other people's stories and help by listening to them, have them feel heard, and assist them in understanding the problems they are encountering and then problem solve. It is one of the greatest experiences to help someone gain insight into their problems, provide support, see them make changes, and celebrate with them when the achieve their goals."*

In addition to being the Substance Abuse Prevention Program Coordinator, Vernalynne also has extensive experience in providing therapy for families dealing with acculturation issues.

Melissa works at MAHA as a mental health counselor and the Mental Health Program Manager. She has years of experience in providing therapy to individuals and families in the Asian community.[224]

I was able to sit down with them during their lunch break to get their expertise and personal experiences of working with intergenerational Asian Americans, particularly immigrant parents and their American born children.

When providing therapy, Melissa explained that some clients (Asian youth) prefer to speak with her alone while others do not mind bringing their parent(s) into the conversation. "Even during therapy sessions, some parents still don't know what therapy is. They think it's something to help their kids in terms of educational purposes," Melissa explained. And when asked about outreach work, Melissa expressed that the mental health program does not advertise their services as therapy sessions, partially due to the stigma and partly because of the lack of understanding of the term from the parents' side. Therefore, they advertise mental health services as being related to education, to help their child do better in school.

While this method could raise ethical concerns on the approach being utilized by the program in order to provide mental health services to this community, the method is not

---

224 Midwest Asian Health Association, "About Us."

uncommon. For example, a similar outreach and recruitment strategy is used by Amy Wang, the program manager at the Asian Health Coalition. In an interview with Amy, she elaborated that "you have to do it kind of covertly" and explain to the parents that the services are to support the students.

In the same in-person interview with Amy, she shared that her parents are engineers and data analysts working for big corporate companies and growing up, provided her with a really good life. Throughout college, as she explored the different majors, she realized that she "really cared about how systems are, how systems of oppression gets built up, and how they keep going. And even though…masses of people are being treated in a bad way, we…don't actually get together and do anything about it."

For both Amy and me, working or volunteering at non-profit organizations has helped us to realize the volume of backstage work that is needed to keep these organizations afloat. We want to go into non-profit organizations with the goal of providing equality and equity to the underserved communities but overlooked the amount of work (e.g., grant writing) needed to receive the funding and the lack of funding available to various initiatives. For example, in recent years, there has been a huge increase in the amount of funding to combat the opioid crisis but meager amounts of funding for mental health services.

Amy shared that although there is funding to fight the rising opioid crisis, this type of funding is not helpful in the Asian community. The abundance of funding for the opioid crisis may be linked to institutional racism that influences the allocation of resources among many other areas.

Recent studies by Taylor N. Santoro and Jonathon D. Santoro (2018) and Joseph Friedman et al. (2019) revealed that ingrained institutional bias may be one of the major factors to the prevalence and the staggering rate of opioid crisis in Caucasian Americans.[225],[226] For example, an analysis by Santoro, T. N. and Santoro J. D. (2018) of the 2016 data on the number of Americans dying from drug overdoses found that the percentage of "Caucasians who died from an opioid-related overdose was 79%, but only 10% for the non-Caucasian minorities, identifying an alarmingly discrepant racial profile of opioid users in the United States."[227] This finding is supported by findings from Joseph Friedman

---

225 Taylor N. Santoro and Jonathon D. Santoro, "Racial Bias in the US Opioid Epidemic: A Review of the History of Systemic Bias and Implications for Care," *Cureus* 10, no. 12 (2018): e3733.

226 Joseph Friedman et al., "Prescription of Opioids and Other Controlled Medications in California," *JAMA Internal Medicine* 179, no. 4 (2019): 467–476.

227 Taylor N. Santoro and Jonathon D. Santoro, "Racial Bias in the US Opioid Epidemic: A Review of the History of Systemic Bias and Implications for Care," *Cureus* 10, no. 12 (2018): e3733.

et al. (2019).[228] Their study revealed data showing that from 2011–2015, opioid overdose deaths were concentrated in lower income and mostly Caucasian areas of California and has a "10-fold difference in overdose rates across the race and ethnicity-income gradient."[229]

While there is no doubt that the opioid crisis is a complex issue, it is difficult to ignore studies such as these, where racial profiles seem to influence the amount of and who the opioid prescriptions are written for and who they are not and indirectly, where the resources and government funding are going towards.

Based on Amy's experience, many Asian youths, especially those living in the inner city of Chicago, they are finding outlets from drinking alcohol, not drugs or even e-cigarettes. Therefore, funding to combat the opioid crisis does little good for the Asian American community, leading to limited funding for programs that will actually be beneficial for the community.

Despite the limited funding, Amy has selflessly donated her own time to work on the mental health needs of the

---

228 Joseph Friedman et al., "Prescription of Opioids and Other Controlled Medications in California," *JAMA Internal Medicine* 179, no. 4 (2019): 467–476.
229 Ibid.

community: reaching out and putting together a mental health panel, communicating with parents through WeChat (a widely used smartphone app similar to WhatsApp or a messaging application), and more recently organizing a Parent Mentor Program at Haines and Ward Elementary Schools in the city. Although still at its infancy, one of the objectives of the Parent Mentor Program is to educate parents on improving communication with their children and mental disorders without explicitly advertising it as what it truly is. Amy shared, "Even when I was doing that mental health panel, I didn't say anything about mental health" and instead explained it to be a holistic educational session focused on the whole "body and soul."

While not all Asian parents are cynical of mental illnesses, many still are. But for some Asian parents, the idea of holistic health and Qi or internally circulating energy is a concept that has been long embedded into the culture and is better understood.

Some may argue that these outreach strategies may seem unethical because the parents do not know what therapies are or that they really are being educated on mental health rather than holistic health. Providing therapy is a relatively new concept in many Asian countries, especially for parents like mine who are immigrants that hailed from the villages and barely graduated from elementary schools. So the most effective way to explain why an illness that cannot be phys-ically seen (unlike a broken bone) still needs to be treated. But holistic health does because it includes healing from the inside, restoring and strengthening the Qi. Therefore, instead of frightening the parents with a concept that they cannot fully understand yet, individuals like Melissa and Amy implement cultural competency by explaining mental illnesses in a manner that is familiar and that can be better understood by them.

The resistance against mental disorder treatments is not exclusive to the older generation. Amy shared her own jour-ney with mental health:

> *"My mother's side of the family has a history of depres-sion and anxiety. I've lived with it all my life…I knew that these were real diagnosis but I thought since they are mood disorders, they're mental disorders. I can then mentally train myself out of it or receive mental training to come out of it…So for a very long time, I was resistant to the idea of psycho medical treat-ments…But because of my father's side of the fam-ily and they were always like 'this is situation, this is a mood disorder and you just need to walk out of this knot that you've tied yourself in' and I still actually struggle with the two different sides. My mother, on the other hand, because she comes from this family*

background, and she does take medication herself,
she says 'why do you not believe in science? There is
a chemical imbalance in your brain that these med-
ications and these treatments are designed to help.'"

Her mother proceeded to explain that if someone had cancer or a collapsed lung, they surely would not refuse treatment, so why would Amy or anyone else struggling with a mental illness deny themselves life-changing treatments?

Because you can't see mental disorders.

No blood draw or medical tests outside of psychological assessments can confirm or deny the long list of mental disorders in existence. With a broken limb, there is an x-ray; for high blood sugar, there is the blood glucose test; but for depression, for example, the person is physically functional in the eyes of the public, even if the illness is very much real. It's just that we can't see it as we can with torn skin. But just because we can't see it with the current medical technology that we have it doesn't mean that mental illnesses don't exist.

From a different perspective but of a similar idea, Jennifer Cheang of Mental Health America observed that, "Serious chronic health conditions like heart disease or diabetes or cancer...you don't wait until they get to stage 4 before you start treating" and instead healthcare providers and individuals focus on prevention, nutrition, and lifestyle choices. Why should it be any different with mental disorders?

B4Stage4 is helping to change the way our society views the path for preventative health for mental health because as Jennifer asserted, "Everybody has mental health, it's not just people living with mental illnesses."

B4Stage4 stages mental health conditions into 4 stages based on severity with stage 1 being mild and stage 4 being most severe.[230] According to Mental Health America's staging chart, stage 1 includes mild signs and symptoms where the person is beginning to show signs and symptoms of a mental health condition but is able to complete normal daily tasks, though sensing that something is not right.[231] Stage 2 begins when the person experiences increased occurrence and more severe symptoms with increased difficulty to maintain and carry out personal responsibilities as it becomes more challenging to ignore symptoms that may be growing in intensity or length of time.[232] Stage 3 starts when there is a worsening or recurrence of symptoms with disruption of routines/responsibilities, a loss of control over daily routines of life, and or responsibilities as the symptoms continue

230 Mental Health America, "B4Stage4: Changing the Way We Think About Mental Health," *Mental Health America* (Accessed March, 2019).
231 Ibid.
232 Ibid.

to grow in severity.[233] Stage 4 presents with persistent and potentially life-threatening symptoms for an extended period and increasing severity of symptoms that may culminate in breakdown and hospitalization; and in extreme cases, when left untreated, suicide.[234]

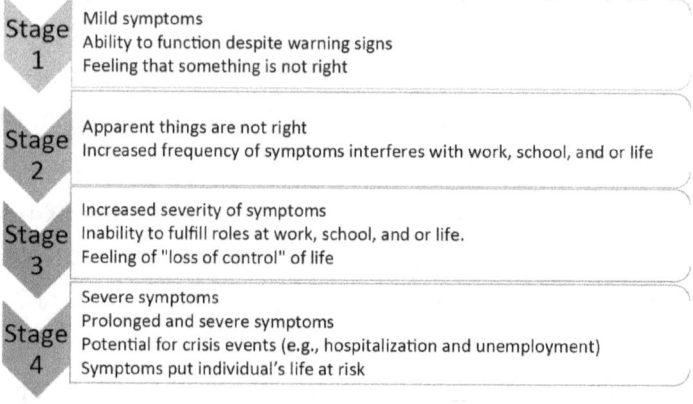

Figure 1: B4Stage4, adapted from Mental Health America.[235]

We need to turn away from the outdated mindset of treating mental illnesses as an acute illness and instead see it as being on a continuum of wellness. But how do we work with non-profit organizations and Asian American communities to educate health care professionals, parents, families, and affected individuals to reduce the stigma against mental

---

233 Ibid.
234 Ibid.
235 Ibid.

disorders and arm them with the tools to detect the early onset of mental illnesses before it goes beyond stage 1 or 2?

It requires changes on the local and system level. We need more people from the community to share their stories because voices are louder than numbers and figures. The voices tell stories that bring their experiences to life and help those in similar situations understand that they are not alone in dealing with mental illnesses. This is supported by Dr. Richard Nakamura, who had a thirty-nine year career at the National Institute of Health, previously served as the director of the Center for Scientific Review (CSR), and held numerous leadership positions, including being the former National Institute of Mental Health's (NIMH) scientific director.[236]

In a phone interview with Dr. Nakamura, he explained that in addition to encouraging more Asian Americans to go into the field of mental health, we need more individuals to, "go out and be willing to talk to groups and communities about their experiences and about the value of treatment of intervention and the importance of family and peer support." In an earlier chapter, Dr. Nakamura shared stories from his family, initially through a video interview through

236 Francis S. Collins, "Statement on the retirement of Dr. Richard Nakamura," National Institutes of Health, April 18, 2018 (Accessed February 20, 2019).

the National Institute of Mental Health, of succeeding in the face of mental illnesses. In addition to family and peer support, Dr. Nakamura is a strong advocate for researching the causes and treatments of various mental illnesses.

"My goal is to advocate on behalf of effective treatment for those with mental illnesses and continued research to refine treatments. It has been a hard road and many treatments don't work for any people, but I think we're developing stronger understandings and the advent of some forms of treatment, like ketamine, that are immediately effective on those with depression is a sign that we are finally understanding more about disorder," stated Dr. Nakamura. He went on to elaborate that in addition to continued research findings on forms of treatments, imaging, and genetic tests are also beginning to reveal differences in the brains of those with mental health conditions, thus supporting the emerging scientific belief that there are physical changes in the brain that underlies some mental disorders.

Despite recent discoveries in the physiologic link between mental disorders and changes in the brain, more research is needed to increase knowledge in the field of mental health and neuroscience in order to improve and expand on treatment options. However, funding for research largely comes from the federal government and often fluctuates from year to year.

This is illustrated in the Substance Abuse and Mental Health Services Administration's (SAMHSA) 2016–2018 budget overview.[237]

SAMHSA 2016–2018 Budget Overview
(Dollars in Million)

Program/Service	2016	2017	2018	Δ 2017–2018
Community Mental Health Services Block Grant	553	532	416	↓ 116
Suicide Prevention Programs	60	60	60	0
Health Surveillance	47	47	34	↓ 13
Public Awareness and Support	16	16	12	↓ 4
Protection and Advocacy for Individuals with Mental Illness	36	36	36	0
Public Health Services (PHS) Evaluation Funds	-134	-133	-120	↑ 13

Table 1: Adapted from SAMHSA Office of Budget, 2017.[238]

It wasn't until as recently as 2018 that the federal government began to take mental health more seriously and provide the

---

237 Office of Budget, "HHS FY 2018 Budget in Brief—SAMHSA," *HHS. gov.* (Accessed June 12, 2019).

238 Ibid.

much needed funding for research of mental disorders, community service support, and outreach efforts.

In the interview, Dr. Nakamura commented that "in the last 12 or 13 years, the funding rate for research in all areas was extremely low" but "thanks to Congress's generosity... right now within the NIMH, funding has risen to about 25% of applications being awarded." The National Alliance on Mental Illness (NAMI) also applauded the increase in federal funding of mental health services and related supports.[239] NAMI highlighted major areas of funding including $306 million for mental health programs to SAMHSA; $160 million for the Community Mental Health Block Grant (MHBG); $109.8 million increase of funding for the NIMH; and an overall of $3 billion increase in funding for the National Institutes of Health (NIH).[240] The funds will go toward mental health services such as early intervention, research, and housing for individuals with disabilities and the homeless among others.[241]

While celebrating these victories, we must continue to advocate for the federal government to continue to increase

---

239 National Alliance on Mental Illness, "NAMI Celebrates Mental Health Victories In Federal Funding Bill," *NAMI* (Accessed June 12, 2019).
240 Ibid.
241 Ibid.

funding or at least maintain the amount of funding for mental health services and research.

A country is only as strong as its people, so it is only logical for the government to invest in the health of its citizens and to recognize that health is inclusive of mental health and should be seen and treated as any other health illnesses. Mental illnesses should not be reduced to numbers and percentages because each number—each story—is a cry for help. Through storytelling from individuals living with mental illnesses or those with loved ones with mental disorders, we can help bring the numbers to life.

CHAPTER 10:

WHAT'S NEXT?

———

In the introduction chapter, I opened up the book with the question, "What do you want to be when you grow up?"

If someone were to ask me the same question today, I would not know how to answer the question. In a strange way, I see the world filled with a greater number of possibilities than I did as a child. As a child, my world was confined to the mile radius between my parents' Chinese restaurant, my schools, and our apartment. But as an adult, I realize that I am my own person and I have the power to steer my life in the direction that I (not my parents) want to.

My parents, likely similar to many immigrant parents, struggled with and continue to find difficulty in trying to communicate effectively with their children, who are now seen in their eyes as only half-Asian because of the contrasting cultural values and mindset. This differing mindset is blatantly apparent in the Asian parents' lack of understanding of the concept of mental health. But it's not just Asian parents, the stigma against mental illnesses is pervasive in the greater Asian communities as well.

Even with an increasing understanding of the brain and with more and more evidence from the scientific community on the relationship between the physiology of the brain and mental disorders, Asian communities still find it challenging to accept the existence of mental illnesses.

The goals of the book were to not only advocate for the mental health needs of Asian Americans but also to reduce the stigma against mental illnesses in the community through the sharing of personal stories from Asian Americans. The book was written *not* as a self-help book but as a book that lends itself as a platform to present the stories of Asian Americans who would otherwise not have been able to share their experiences with mental disorders. Furthermore, including interviews with experts in the field and those doing the groundwork helps to shed light on the system level challenges that these individuals face as they continue to push forward selflessly.

My hope is that as more Asian Americans come forward and share their stories, the society will come to recognize the prevalence of mental illnesses in this community. An equally important recognition would be for Asian parents to understand that mental disorders do exist. Their children need their support and love more than having their college tuitions paid and to encourage the parents to prioritize their children over the fear of embarrassment and losing face. The road to recovery takes a tremendous amount of courage and will. Having a supportive group of family and friends will certainly provide individuals with the much needed strength to keep on fighting.

There is still so much work that needs to be done as an individual, as a community, and as a society. But with patience and the right mindset, we can work together to improve the experiences of Asian Americans with mental disorders and their individual journeys to recovery.

So what kind of changes do these experts hope to see in the next five to ten years in terms of mental health among Asian Americans? Some of the most common answers were to see more Asian American mental health providers and for more individuals from the community to seek out the care they need and deserve.

For Alexis Gao, who is in her last year of graduate school and soon to receive her PsyD in clinical psychology, she stated:

> *"I want to see a growing population of AAPI individuals attending graduate school for Psychology because they too want to shatter glass ceilings. I want to see more of the AAPI community at conferences that are not just Asian American Psychology Association conference. I once went to the National Academy of Neuropsychology conference and I only saw a handful of AAPI individuals. I want more classes about Asian American and Pacific Islander cultures and Psychology, but to stop generalizing the whole community because AAPI is made up of over hundreds of cultures."*

Ellen S., a clinical psychologist who has worked with Asian Americans, also added:

> *"I'm hoping that the parents, especially immigrants, are more open to getting treatment. I also hope that we have more bi-lingual clinicians, especially for Asians from less represented countries like Sri Lanka or Bangladesh."*

And for Vernalynne, she shared:

"I hope to see less stigma and more openness to talk about mental illness in the Asian community. I hope to see more Asian American providers/clinicians to provide services to the Asian American community in the desired Asian language. I also want more Asian community organization addressing education about mental health for the Asian American community. I want more workshops for Asian American parents to learn about the balance between positive emotional health and educational/professional success for their youth and their families. These workshops will also provide parents how to best support their youth and themselves with creating well-rounded person with a high IQ and EQ."

We need more representation in the media in sharing our experiences and in the field of mental health. As Alexis explained, we need to be part of the movement to shatter the glass ceilings and to debunk the model minority myth.

Today, many more Asian Americans than in the past are coming forward and have bravely shared some of the most painful moments of their lives with the world because their stories help others know that they are not alone in their struggle against mental health. But we know that there are many more stories out there that have not been told because of the continuing stigma within the Asian community.

In order to transform the way mental health is viewed and the way mental health services are being accessed and delivered, we need to speak up about the issues that matter to our communities the most because if we don't speak up, no one will. Know that however big or small our contributions are every action leaves behind an imprint.

So, speak up!

WORKS REFERENCED

INTRODUCTION

HHS.gov. "Mental Health and Asian Americans." *U.S. Department of Health and Human Services Office of Minority Health.* Accessed March 2019. https://minorityhealth.hhs.gov/omh/browse.aspx?lvl=4&lvlid=54.

Nishi, Koko. "Mental Health Among Asian-Americans." *American Psychological Association.* Accessed March 2019. https://www.apa.org/pi/oema/resources/ethnicity-health/asian-american/article-mental-health.

Pew Research Center. "Key Facts About Asian Americans, A Diverse And Growing Population." *Pew Research Cen-*

ter. September 8, 2017. https://www.pewresearch.org/fact-tank/2017/09/08/key-facts-about-asian-americans/.

CHAPTER 1

Chen, Stacy. "New Generation of Asian American Women are Fighting to Normalize Mental Health Treatment." *Good Morning America.* Accessed April 19, 2019. https://www.goodmorningamerica.com/wellness/story/generation-asian-american-women-fighting-normalize-mental-health-57651825.

"Saving Face in China." *The International Herald Tribune.* December 13, 2010. https://www.nytimes.com/2010/12/14/business/global/14iht-busnav14.html.

Yu, Ning. "What Does Our Face Mean to Us?" *Pragmatics & Cognition* 9, no. 1 (2001): 1-36, https://web.archive.org/web/20110614054308/http://faculty-staff.ou.edu/Y/Ning.Yu-1/Yu-2001.pdf.

CHAPTER 2

Asian Americans In The Law. "The Model Minority Myth: Highlighting Key Stories About the Profession You May Have Missed." *Asian Americans In The Law* 5, no. 1 (2018).

Access March 2019). https://thepractice.law.harvard.edu/
article/the-model-minority-myth/.

Budiman, Abby, Anthony, Cilluffo, and Neil G. Ruiz, "Key
Facts About Asian Origin Groups in the U.S." *Pew
Research Center*. May 22 2019. https://www.pewresearch.
org/fact-tank/2019/05/22/key-facts-about-asian-origin-
groups-in-the-u-s/.

Charles, Brian. "Study Sponsored by Assemblyman Mike
Eng Shows Asian Community Overlooked." *The Sun*.
December 2, 2010. https://www.sbsun.com/2010/12/02/
study-sponsored-by-assemblyman-mike-eng-shows-
asian-community-overlooked/.

Cheang, Jennifer. "Asian American Mental Health and
the 'Model Minority' Myth." *Mental Health America*.
May 7, 2018. https://www.mentalhealthamerica.net/blog/
asian-american-mental-health-and-%E2%80%98mod-
el-minority%E2%80%99-myth.

Fuchs, Chris. "Behind the 'Model Minority' Myth: Why the
'Studious Asian' Stereotype Hurts." *NBC News*. August
22, 2017. https://www.nbcnews.com/news/asian-america/
behind-model-minority-myth-why-studious-asian-ste-
reotype-hurts-n792926.

Hall Nagayama, Gordon C. and Alicia Yee. "U.S. Mental Health Policy: Addressing the Neglect of Asian Americans." *Asian American Journal of Psychology* 3, no. 3 (2012): 181-193.

HHS.gov. "Mental Health and Asian Americans." *U.S. Department of Health and Human Services Office of Minority Health.* Accessed March 2019. https://minorityhealth.hhs.gov/omh/browse.aspx?lvl=4&lvlid=54.

Kat Chow. "Model Minority' Myth Again Used as a Racial Wedge Between Asians and Blacks." *NPR.* April 19, 2017. https://www.npr.org/sections/codeswitch/2017/04/19/524571669/model-minority-myth-again-used-as-a-racial-wedge-between-asians-and-blacks.

Nishi, Koko. "Mental Health Among Asian-Americans." *American Psychological Association.* Accessed March 2019. https://www.apa.org/pi/oema/resources/ethnicity-health/asian-american/article-mental-health.

Vespa, Jonathan, David M. Armstrong, and Lauren Medina. "Demographic Turning Points for the United States: Population Projections for 2020 To 2060." *United States Census Bureau.* March 2018. https://www.census.gov/content/dam/Census/library/publications/2018/demo/P25_1144.pdf.

CHAPTER 3

"About." *Erasing Shame* (blog). n.d., https://erasingshame.com/about/.

Elaine Chong. "Chinese Takeaway Kids: What's it Like to Grow Up in One?" *BBC News.* Accessed January 26, 2019. https://www.bbc.com/news/av/stories-47007812/chinese-takeaway-kids-what-s-it-like-to-grow-up-in-one.

"Korean American Pressures to Be Perfect." *Erasing Shame* (blog). July 5, 2018, https://erasingshame.com/korean-american-pressures-to-be-perfect/.

Maddoux Rowland. "Asian Pacific American Heritage Month Speaker Discusses Mental Health." *Central Michigan Life.* Accessed March 21, 2019. http://www.cm-life.com/article/2019/03/asian-pacific-american-heritage-month-speaker-jr-kuo.

Mental Health America. "B4Stage4: Changing the Way We Think About Mental Health." *Mental Health America.* Accessed March 2019. https://www.mhanational.org/b4stage4-changing-way-we-think-about-mental-health.

CHAPTER 4

Asian Coalition 亞洲聯盟. "Mike Eng Shares His Own Stories of Why He Cares About Mental Health & Speaking Out About Mental Illness." *Facebook*. 2016. https://www.facebook.com/pg/AsianCoalition/videos/?ref=page_internal.

Each Mind Matters. "Emily Wu Truong in Each Mind Matter's Anti-Stigma Campaign." *YouTube*. October 1, 2014. https://www.youtube.com/watch?v=kcBw53dSp2c.

Emily Wu Truong. "Emily Wu Truong 吳怡萱." *Facebook*. https://www.facebook.com/MLEWu/.

Emily Wu Truong. "The Positive Side of Thinking About Mental Health." *TEDx Talks*. July 11, 2017. https://www.youtube.com/watch?v=Beugk4Po3d4.

"Mike Eng." *Facebook*. https://www.facebook.com/mike.eng/?fref=nf.

"Mike Eng." *Linkedin*. https://www.linkedin.com/in/mike-eng-69a60b5/.

CHAPTER 5

Collins, Francis S. "Statement on the Retirement of Dr. Richard Nakamura." *National Institutes of Health.* April 18, 2018. https://www.nih.gov/about-nih/who-we-are/nih-director/statements/statement-retirement-dr-richard-nakamura.

Mental Health America. "Recovery is a Journey." *Mental Health America.* Accessed June 2019. https://www.mhanational.org/recovery-journey.

CHAPTER 6

Asian Community Mental Health Services. "ACMHS [PDF file]." *ACMHS.* Accessed June 2019. http://www.acmhs.org/wp-content/uploads/Resumes-Color-Logo-and-BnW-Photo-NO-LOPEZ.pdf.

Gaw, Albert. "Working with Asian American Patients." *American Psychiatric Association.* Accessed June 2019. https://www.psychiatry.org/psychiatrists/cultural-competency/education/best-practice-highlights/working-with-asian-american-patients.

Hari, Riitta. "From Brain—Environment Connections to Temporal Dynamics and Social Interaction: Principles of Human Brain Function." *Neuron* 94, no. 5 (2017): 1033-1039. https://doi.org/10.1016/j.neuron.2017.04.007.

Lam, Vivian. "'We Know Very Little About the Brain': Experts Outline Challenges in Neuroscience." *Stanford Medicine: Scope.* November 2016. https://scopeblog.stanford.edu/2016/11/08/challenges-in-neuroscience-in-the-21st-century/.

Masdeu, Joseph C. "Neuroimaging in Psychiatric Disorders." *Neurotherapeutics: the Journal of the American Society for Experimental NeuroTherapeutics,* 8, no. 1 (2011): 93–102.

Pattani, Aneri. "She Kept Losing Her Eyesight, and No One Knew Why. Then a Doctor Asked About Her Mental Health." *The Philadelphia Inquirer.* January 2019.

https://www.inquirer.com/health/asian-american-mental-illness-somatic-symptoms-diana-chao-20190122.html.

Quinn, Cristina. "Mass. Study Shows Major Mental Healthcare Disparity Between Whites And Asian-Americans." *WGBH News.* April, 2018. https://www.wgbh.org/news/2018/04/25/news/mass-study-shows-major-mental-healthcare-disparity-between-whites-and-asian.

Radiological Society of North America. "MRI Uncovers Brain Abnormalities in People With Depression, Anxiety." *ScienceDaily.* November 2017. https://www.sciencedaily.com/releases/2017/11/171120085448.htm.

"Riitta Hari." *Mendeley.* Accessed June 2019. https://www.mendeley.com/profiles/riitta-hari/.

Stanford Medicine. "Lu Chen," *Stanford Medicine: CAP Profiles.* Accessed June 2019. https://med.stanford.edu/profiles/lu-chen.

Weir, Kirsten. "The Roots of Mental Illness: How Much of Mental Illness Can the Biology of the Brain Explain?" *American Psychological Association* 43, no. 6 (2012): 30. https://www.apa.org/monitor/2012/06/roots.

Yeung, Albert and Raymond Kam. "Recognizing and Treating Depression in Asian Americans." *Psychiatric Times* 23, no. 14 (2006). https://www.psychiatrictimes.com/depression/recognizing-and-treating-depression-asian-americans.

CHAPTER 7

Balm Tiger. "Small Tiger Balm White—HR Ointment 10G (0.35 Oz)." Accessed April 2019. https://balmtiger.com/

product/small-tiger-balm-white-hr-ointment-10g-0-35-oz/.

Hall Nagayama, Gordon C. "Interview with Martin Hsia." *PsychRally*. Podcast Audio. October 12, 2017. http://www.psychrallypodcast.com/e/29/.

Substance Abuse and Mental Health Services Administration (SAMHSA). "Mental Health Information: Statistics." *National Institute of Mental Health*. February 2019. https://www.nimh.nih.gov/health/statistics/mental-illness.shtml.

Tanap, Ryann. "Ryann Tanap." *LinkedIn*. Accessed March 2019. https://www.linkedin.com/in/rmtanap/.

Tanap, Ryann. "Why Asian-Americans and Pacific Islanders Don't Go to Therapy." *National Alliance on Mental Illness*. July 24, 2018. https://www.nami.org/Blogs/NAMI-Blog/July-2018/Why-Asian-Americans-and-Pacific-Islanders-Don-t-go.

Tiger Balm. "Tiger Balm Soft." Accessed April 2019. https://www.tigerbalm.com/sg/range/3/range_products/TIGER_BALM_SOFT/.

u/bbaek. "The /r/APS Medicine Cabinet." Accessed April 2019. https://www.reddit.com/r/AsianParentStories/comments/96ofvp/the_raps_medicine_cabinet/.

CHAPTER 8

National Institute of Mental Health (NIMH). "Mental Illness in Stressful Times - An Asian-American Family's Story." *YouTube*. July 28, 2016. https://www.youtube.com/watch?v=usI6PDwMjcw.

Richard Nakamura. "Richard Nakamura." *LinkedIn*. https://www.linkedin.com/in/richard-nakamura-3852246a.

CHAPTER 9

Collins, Francis S. "Statement on the Retirement of Dr. Richard Nakamura." National Institutes of Health. April 18, 2018. https://www.nih.gov/about-nih/who-we-are/nih-director/statements/statement-retirement-dr-richard-nakamura.

Friedman, Joseph et al. "Prescription of Opioids and Other Controlled Medications in California." *JAMA Internal Medicine*, no. 4 (2019): 467-476.

Mental Health America. "B4Stage4: Changing the Way We Think About Mental Health." *Mental Health America.* Accessed March 2019. https://www.mentalhealthamerica. net/b4stage4-changing-way-we-think-about-mental-health.

Midwest Asian Health Association. "About McK-UDOS." http://maha-us.org/substance-abuse-prevention-program/ about-us-2/.

Midwest Asian Health Association. "About Us." http://maha-us. org/about-us/.

Office of Budget. "HHS FY 2018 Budget in Brief – SAMHSA." *HHS.gov.* Accessed June 12, 2019. https://www.hhs.gov/ about/budget/fy2018/budget-in-brief/samhsa/index.html.

Santoro, Taylor N. and Santoro, Jonathon D. "Racial Bias in the US Opioid Epidemic: A Review of the History of Systemic Bias and Implications for Care." *Cureus,* no. 12 (2018): e3733.

CHAPTER 10

National Alliance on Mental Illness. "NAMI Celebrates Mental Health Victories in Federal Funding Bill." *NAMI.* Accessed June 12, 2019. https://www.nami.org/Press-Media/ Press-Releases/2018/NAMI-Celebrates-Mental-Health-Vic- tories-in-Federal.